MW01060537

In the twenty-five years I have wo..... never encountered a colleague who had a better perspective on the college admissions process than Bill Mayher. His extraordinary insights into people enabled him to understand his students (and parents) better than most, and he guided students to evaluate colleges based on the appropriateness of the match rather than the selectivity index. **—Mary Lou W. Bates**
Director of Admissions, Skidmore College

What a well-written, honest book about the process! Families will truly benefit from the years of experience of a true counselor and admissions professional.
—Nancy Hargrave Meislahn
Director of Undergraduate Admissions, Cornell University

This book should be read by every parent whose teenager is about to embark on the college admissions process and by every beginning college counselor. Mr. Mayher's experiences and insightfulness into family dynamics can have a profound effect on those interested in the complexities of the college search. Mr. Mayher, through his anecdotes, will touch the soul of everyone who reads his book and he does so with humor and compassion.
—Lindsay J. Bates
Director of Guidance, John Jay High School, Katonah, N.Y.

Bill Mayher's honest and no-nonsense approach is leavened with illuminating anecdotes that demystify the college process and provide students and parents with a useful guide for managing the task of applying to college.
—Sherrie H. McKenna and Bob Wheeler
former Associate Directors of Admissions, Yale University

A rational how-to manual for exploring and applying to colleges. Bill Mayher confronts head-on the American obsession with image and reputation over true quality and fit with respect to higher education. He urges families to be wary of the marketing tactics used by colleges, to take control of the college admission process, not be controlled by it. **—John L. Mahoney**
Director of Undergraduate Admission, Boston College

Good Luck!
Bill Mayher

THE COLLEGE ADMISSIONS MYSTIQUE

👍 BILL MAYHER 👎

FARRAR, STRAUS AND GIROUX / NEW YORK

A division of Farrar, Straus and Giroux
19 Union Square West, New York 10003

Copyright © 1998 by Bill Mayher
All rights reserved
Distributed in Canada by Douglas & McIntyre Ltd.
Printed in the United States of America
Designed by Abby Kagan
First edition, 1998
5 7 9 11 10 8 6

Library of Congress Cataloging-in-Publication Data
Mayher, Bill, 1941-
    The college admissions mystique /
Bill Mayher. — 1st ed.
        p. cm.
    ISBN 0-374-52513-7 (pbk. : alk. paper)
    1. Universities and colleges—United States—Admission.
    2. Universities and colleges—United States—Entrance requirements.
    I. Title.
LB2351.2.M29 1998
378.1'61'0973—dc21   97-14576

Grateful acknowledgment is made for permission to reprint from the
following: "Unbound Aspirations" by David W. Brennan, *Harvard
Magazine*, September–October 1996. Copyright © 1996 by David W.
Brennan. Reprinted by permission of *Harvard Magazine*. *The College Board
Admissions Testing Program.* Copyright © 1971 by College Entrance Examination Board. Reprinted by permission of The College Board. *None
of the Above* by David Owen. Copyright © 1985 by David Owen. Reprinted
by permission of Houghton Mifflin Co. *Emotional Intelligence* by Daniel
Goleman. Copyright © 1995 by Daniel Goleman. Reprinted by permission
of Bantam Books, a division of Bantam Doubleday Dell Publishing Group,
Inc.

To my wife, Caroline, and my daughter, Jenny—
the best home team a person could ever have

CONTENTS

PREFACE

I wrote this book because I am frustrated by the way the selective college admissions process diminishes so many of our children. We know that when young people set off for college what they need most is self-confidence. Yet the admissions process, by its very nature, conspires to strip self-confidence from too many of our kids. It does this by making not the education but "getting in" the main event. At the precise moment when young people step toward the threshold of adulthood and say, "My dream is to do this thing at that place," responsible adults are compelled by the system to rush forward saying, "But not so fast, young lady, your SATs . . ." or "Wait just a minute, young man, I'm not sure that your class rank . . ."

Given the system in place, we adults have little choice. It

is prudent to warn young people of the realities of selective admissions; we must encourage them to think of strategies and contingencies and compromises. To do otherwise would be irresponsible. Life, after all, is no endless day at Disney World. But it does seem a shame that so many young people head off to college feeling deflated because either they didn't get into the college of their choice or, far more likely, they have already scaled down their choices (as well as their sense of themselves) to meet the "realities" of the selective admissions marketplace. How many of our young people begin the sojourn to adulthood carrying internal passports stamped: "Not Ivy League Material"? It's a shame that we have created a system mandating that, ultimately, almost everybody doesn't get in somewhere—even at the highest echelons of the college pecking order. It may be all right for an athletic shoe manufacturer to push its products by claiming, as one did at the 1996 Olympics, "You didn't win the Silver, you lost the Gold." But it is not footwear we are talking about here; it is our children. We have created a system in which winners "lose." It is a system in which too many kids at Yale spend far too much of their freshman year talking about why they didn't get into Harvard, and too many kids at Dartmouth worry about why they didn't get into Princeton. If these elite students feel wounded and diminished, what about the huge number who thought it was hopeless to try for Yale and Dartmouth to begin with?

These are painful questions without good answers, and, unfortunately, few of us believe that this selective college admissions system is likely to change. As we shall see, this system is too embedded in the national culture and too useful a marketing tool for our most powerful colleges.

This book, therefore, does not presume to change the

system. What it does attempt to do is to help your family change its perception of the system and to understand the peculiar truth that many Americans are more preoccupied with a college's selectivity than they are with its actual quality. You will see why this preoccupation has enabled selective colleges to raise tuitions consistently higher than the consumer price index, even though the number of students with families able to pay these tuitions continues to decline. By poking a little fun at our national obsession with admissions, by revealing the essence of the college admissions mystique, by being a little skeptical, the book shows parents and their children they needn't be whipsawed by what is arguably the most successfully marketed product in American history: a place in the freshman class at a highly selective college. Instead of chasing fashion trends and the vicissitudes of annual rating guides, let's focus on what is best for our children.

To accomplish this I try to engage the reader in a useful conversation on the subject of selective college admissions. How did it get to be the way it is? How do our hopes and fears play into the way it works? How can we see through the marketing clutter and view colleges clearly? How can we develop effective strategies to deal with specific college admissions challenges without giving in to the general hysteria? How can we help our children take charge of the process and, with it, their lives? How can we help them understand that college admissions should never have the power to tell our children who they are? Only they have the power to do that.

The convictions set down in this book were built over a lifetime of work as a college counselor at two of the finest independent schools in the nation: Hackley School in Tarrytown, New York, and Noble and Greenough School in Dedham, Massachusetts. In my years of work in those schools I learned from many people. First among my teachers were the students I counseled. They continuously instructed me about how resilient young people are; they taught me to trust their energy and curiosity; and they showed me that if we could clear a space for honest dialogue between us, there was no situation we couldn't improve. Also among my teachers were the parents of these students. They helped me understand there is never only one way to guide children. They showed me, through the diversity of their own backgrounds, how many ways there are to achieve success in this country. Finally, they taught me to see the lives of their children not simply in terms of the high school to college transition but over the longer haul of a family's life together.

My third set of teachers has been my college counseling colleagues. They are an exceptional group of professionals: intelligent, caring, mature, idealistic. Perhaps the nature of the work explains these qualities. In a job that daily reminds us to keep our humility, our sense of fairness, and our sense of humor at the ready, we probably have little other choice. Beyond these qualities, what makes this group even more extraordinary is the willingness to share ideas and information. Locked away in our separate schools, we could view each other as competitors; instead, we have become colleagues and friends. Without their help and support over many years, I doubt if the book I have written for parents and students at the threshold of college admissions would be as useful as I hope it will be.

THE COLLEGE ADMISSIONS MYSTIQUE

INTRODUCTION

*Mystique: "A complex of transcendental or semi-mystical beliefs
and attitudes directed toward or developing around an object
(as a person, institution, idea, or pursuit) and enhancing
the value or significance of the object by embuing it with
an esoteric truth or meaning."*
—Webster's New International Dictionary

When a family embarks on its college admissions
journey with a son or daughter, the experience
can be bewildering for all concerned. In this unfamiliar and shifting terrain a family can lose its bearings,
fall behind the pace of deadlines, and become so twitchy
that people have trouble being in the same room with each
other. Over my years as a college counselor, however, I have
found that if both parents and students gain a basic understanding of what is really going on in the world of admissions, they will be able to break its fearsome grip, revert to
being at their best, and ultimately be able to make intelligent, comfortable decisions. Building the understanding to
make this possible is my goal.

I hope when you read this book, it feels like a relaxed

conversation with me in my office. With this in mind, Part I is general and theoretical in nature: a look at the broad picture of college admissions and how it fits into contemporary American culture. Part II is an annotated time line providing an overview of what lies ahead for your family in the upcoming admissions year. Parts III, IV, V, and VI present specific cases and strategies to guide you from the initial process of discovering colleges, through the necessary steps in the application phase, to the moment when college news arrives at home. Part VII offers a series of final thoughts, which I hope will stimulate useful and interesting thinking and discussion among you all.

Because parents often take the initiative in college admissions, the book begins by addressing them directly. As the process unfolds and kids become increasingly involved—often taking over completely—I turn the conversation toward them. Hopefully, readers won't be confused or put off as I direct ideas to first one audience and then the other.

After close to thirty years in the business, I still consider the college admissions process to be a worthwhile family adventure. I know it is a process that engenders growth and understanding among all concerned. I also know the college admissions process, if well-done, has the power to make a college career a more fruitful and exciting enterprise. In this journey of yours—one that may well begin with the reading of this book—I wish you all the best of luck.

PART I

THE COLLEGE ADMISSIONS MYSTIQUE

1

COLLEGE LOOMS AHEAD

*You gain strength, courage, and confidence by every experience
in which you really stop and look fear in the face. You are
able to say, "I lived through this horror. I can take the
next thing that comes along." You must do the thing
you think you can not do.*
—Eleanor Roosevelt

The subject of college admissions makes a lot of people
nervous. Somewhere around the time a child turns
sixteen, the world mysteriously divides itself into winners and losers. A sense of judgment day hovers. Young people and their parents line up at sorting chutes feeling
uneasy, as if they were about to be strip-searched. No place
is safe. A high school senior traveling alone on an airplane
is widely regarded as an item of such public property that
the stranger in the next seat feels free to ask the youngster
about his SAT scores or whether he plays basketball or the
oboe. And if this kid even hints that he has a list of colleges,
the stranger will feel free to speculate about which ones he
won't get admitted to. From the sidelines of Little League

games to the dentist's waiting room, self-appointed experts lurk everywhere. The 1920s were famous for cabdrivers who had the last word about stocks; now these cabbies are omniscient about college admissions. For the parents of teenagers, the beach that used to be a relaxing place to read mysteries and watch children scamper at the water's edge is now rife with rumor as people become hysterical about who got in and, worse yet, who didn't. Even business lunches among men, who until recently have pretty much left the educational progress of their children to their wives, can turn in an instant to college admissions talk.

Few middle-class families escape a brush with this dreadful flu, and as the pressure rises, what has been called the parental magnification effect often takes over and blows events in our children's lives out of proportion. (If Joyce scores a goal, she's on her way to the Olympics. If Jim gets a B−, he'll never get into a "good" college.) As the emotional level rises, so does the potential for finger-pointing. We blame the teacher, the coach, the counselor. We blame the wacky kids in the car pool and the dumb music that surely erodes our child's ability to cerebrate at school. We blame ourselves: our darling Jason would surely be a Heifetz and a shoo-in at Harvard if we hadn't let up on those violin lessons in the third grade. We don't have friends on the boards of Ivy League colleges. Our genetic material is deficient, especially those genes having to do with aptitude for foreign languages and chemistry. In the dead of night we can even find ourselves wishing, no matter how much we love our kids exactly the way they are, that they were a bit flashier.

Blindsided by these emotions, we feel vulnerable and exposed. As Michael Thompson, a Boston psychologist who often treats families in the throes of the college admissions sickness, writes, "It can make normal people act quite nutty and nutty people act quite crazy." And it doesn't help that most of our friends find themselves in the same spot; in the big college scramble, we have slipped into competition even with them.

As the clock ticks toward April of senior year, Thanksgiving dinner with the relatives can be the worst. In a typical scene—grandparents, aunts, and uncles, everyone chatting and reaching for another dab of cranberry sauce—all of a sudden someone asks Justin, the high school senior down at the other end of the table, where he plans to apply to college. On the surface it's an innocent question, but the silence that cuts like a blade across the table indicates that maybe it isn't. Heads pivot Justin's way; he feels all eyes on him. Only a year or two ago, he was over at the kids' table trying to get one of his cousins to eat a giblet. Now he is called to the stand, asked to publicly declare his competence to a jury of relatives and in-laws, some of whom may not be so impartial, some of whom might be hoping Justin is not as smart as their own kid.

The pressure he feels down there at the other end of the table probably explains why so many of our children confront the college admissions situation either with spectacular acts of neglect or by just jumping up and leaving the room altogether when parents bring it up. Such reluctance to deal with the subject makes parenting a ticklish job and can leave us puzzled and angry. Here we are about to spend a very large sum of money to guarantee the future happiness and security of our kids and they won't even discuss the subject. No matter how hard we try, there never seems to be a "right" time to talk.

Of course, kids see it differently. They seem incapable of regarding college as four years of uninterrupted intellectual stimulation in some temple of learning that serves hot meals regularly and presents rich opportunities for games, movies, beer parties, all-night talk, and even romance. Locked in the pressure cooker of late adolescence, all they see is the gateway, the rejection machinery of college, which will snatch them up by the neck and speed them down to some dissection table where they will be cut open, discussed by total strangers, and then, quite probably, deselected in front of their entire known world. With this nightmare in mind, quite naturally they are not eager to get started.

So right at the beginning of the great life adventure of college admissions, families find themselves locked in a tense stalemate. Parents, knowing there is a job to do, lunge ahead. Kids, scared they might not live up to expectations held by themselves or others, burrow deeper into their own misgivings.

Before we attempt remedies, let's take a closer look at the subject of college admissions craziness in the hopes that a little historical perspective might help everyone to relax.

2

TAIL FINS AND IVY WALLS

Every age has its obsessions, its ziggurats and cata-combs, celestial highways and roads to hell, its reli-quaries and hula hoops. While it's always entertaining to cluck and chuckle as unassailable dogmas of the past are transmuted into picturesque superstitions, it's also in-triguing to speculate about which of our current cultural icons and fixations will seem like a hoot to our great-grandchildren.

Already, for example, the bright light of historical per-spective has put the car culture of the 1950s and its tail fin madness under our amused scrutiny. This was the era of the extreme annual style change, when automobile dealers cov-ered their showroom windows with paper until the day the new models were officially revealed to a curious and fawning public. In those days, everything about the manufacture and marketing of new cars—their look, the status they conferred, even their smell—coalesced into a major organizing principle of American economic and social life, which now looks about as gaudy and tinny as the cars that rolled out of Detroit factories.

Although America has had a long and fabled love affair with the automobile, this passion hit new levels of intensity in the 1950s. As the decade began, the automobile industry, long shackled by the Great Depression and then World War II, was at last free to give people what they wanted: access to cars. And these new cars would not be frugal, utilitarian machines like Henry Ford's Model T. These new beauties— stretched-out, lowered-down, and powered by high-compression engines—not only would express a nation's dreams, but also would tell the world that the man in the driver's seat (and it was surely a man in those days) had earned a well-deserved place for himself on the main highway of American life.

People became the cars they drove, and to highlight this fusion General Motors composed an ascending hierarchy of models that went from Chevrolet to Pontiac to Oldsmobile to Buick, all the way to Cadillac. Soon Chrysler, with their Plymouth-Dodge-Chrysler-Imperial slate, and Ford, with a Mercury-Lincoln-Continental line, followed suit with their own bevies of cars. The corporate strategy would be to initially win the customer's lifelong loyalty and then reward that loyalty with increasingly elaborate and expensive cars as his career progressed, as it surely would. Complementing this dynamic hierarchy was the concept of annual style change, which guaranteed that when you drove a new car, people would be sure to notice its newness.

For the sake of argument, one can maintain that the current fascination middle-class American culture has with selective college admissions is nearly as lavish as that of the '50s car culture. In a generation or two, it will become clear how much we have invested in the madness surrounding selective admissions and how much we have lost.

In the world of selective college admissions, the analogy to the automotive status hierarchy is the rear-window college decal. If the driver of a Buick in the '50s was instantly recognizable as a solid member of the postwar haute bourgeoisie—a banker, perhaps—then the driver of a car with a Princeton decal on the back window in our own time is presumed to be high in the pecking order of contemporary national life; higher, certainly, than the driver of a car with a Lafayette sticker.

In my work as a college counselor, I have long been impressed with how carefully calibrated the public's sense of college prestige has become—how rarely, for example, a senior in high school, with a group of acceptances in hand, fails to choose the most prestigious college to attend. Once I asked Andrew, a student who was known for his impeccable sense of which college ranked where, how he had managed to internalize the pecking order of colleges with such precision. He told me he had first become aware of college names on ski trips. As his family drove from Boston to ski areas at Stowe or Killington, his parents often made note of college decals on the rear windows of passing station wagons. For Andrew's parents, the decals served as family report cards posted on car windows for the world to see and discuss. When there was a group of stickers on a window, the animated discussion of nuances lasted for miles. (Did that Dartmouth sticker among a group of "safety" schools represent a genetic anomaly or the presence of a hockey player in the family?) This front-seat game kept the grown-ups busy for hours.

Like legends internalized by children around the cooking fires of traditional peoples, these words sunk in deep. As Andrew's parents deconstructed fresh constellations of decals and computed their prestige quotient against the model of car they were affixed to, Andrew learned to imagine that the people riding in cars proclaiming Amherst or Duke looked like the right kind of family, while those with other college labels Andrew had trouble remembering from one trip to the next, didn't. From the time he was a little boy, before he knew algebra or could conjugate a single verb in a foreign language, Andrew was made aware of the potency of college names, spoken out in hushed liturgical tones, as the family swept along the snowy highways of his childhood.

Another similarity between '50s cars and college admissions is the puzzling lack of concern on the part of consumers as to how they work, about what actually goes on under the hood, so to speak, of either cars or colleges. No one bothered much with how cars performed, and as the decade progressed, in recompense for this carelessness, Detroit models grew increasingly less dependable (even as their fins got longer). But it didn't affect sales, because what mattered was how cars made their drivers feel.

A selective admissions system in which desirability is based on prestige is analogous to this. If a college is prestigious enough, if its decal telegraphs enough power, then it is, ipso facto, the best college. We needn't inquire further into its actual performance, or even whether its primary mission is to educate undergraduates. Everything will be taken care of by the magic elixir of prestige. The self-esteem of any student lucky enough to be accepted will rocket ever upward, and the world, it is assumed by everyone involved, will forever want to befriend, hire, marry, and live happily ever after with what must be a surefire winner.

With both cars and colleges, there is a very American theology of winning and losing. In each, the struggle to achieve either a fancy car or a fancy college becomes a map by which to navigate the ambiguities of contemporary life. In the '50s, good people drove Oldsmobiles, better people drove Buicks, and the best people drove Cadillacs. In the struggle for places in top colleges, we believe that quality is rewarded and recognized just as clearly.

Looking back over the excesses of the 1950s, we now see the price of this theology. For one thing, our lack of critical thinking about car quality led to the production of increasingly shoddy models, which ultimately opened the door to foreign competition. The importation of the Volkswagen Beetle broke the ice. That modern-day recapitulation of the Model T penetrated the U.S. market with so few amenities that the first models didn't even have gas gauges. But the Beetle was dependable and got good gas mileage, so it won a place in the American market. After a half-hearted salvo of Pintos and Corvairs was fired into the small-car market, Detroit went back to the old formula, churning out "gas-guzzling behemoths," confident that its market niche at the heart of American life was ever secure. But when the Arab oil embargo put fuel consumption on the front burner, a flood of German, Japanese, and even Korean imports permanently altered our manufacturing hegemony in the world economy and our balance of trade. For all their classic kookiness, maybe those '50s cars weren't so funny after all.

Although the American system of higher education is still correctly regarded as the world's most potent, the fact that its consumers at the undergraduate level continue to gobble up its wares with such uncritical enthusiasm might give us pause. We should look critically at the fact that our most desirable and prestigious universities often act as if their undergraduate colleges are merely picturesque sideshows, useful for fund-raising and football, while the real performance—research grants, and contracts (the stuff the faculty cares about)—happens under the big tops of their graduate schools.

Reviewing Charles Clotfelter's book *Buying the Best* in *Harvard Magazine* in 1996, David W. Brennan reports: "For regular-rank faculty (those holding tenured or tenure track appointments), teaching loads in the representative humanities departments at Duke fell from 5.6 courses in the 1976–77 academic year to 4.2 in 1991–92; from 4.3 courses to 3.6 in the social sciences departments; and from 3.4 courses to 2.5 in the natural sciences departments . . . At Harvard, in the departments reviewed, the course load in the humanities remained stable at 2.8 per year, but declined in social sciences from 3.6 to 2.5, and in the natural sciences from 1.7 to 1.6." Brennan then points out an interesting comparison between research universities and colleges (in this case Carleton) that Clotfelter's research reveals: "By the 1991–92 academic year, for example, the average class size in the social science department was 80 at Duke, 242 at Harvard, 38 at Chicago, and 24 at Carleton. At Duke, 72 percent of the courses in that discipline were taught by regular-rank faculty, compared to only 48 percent at Harvard and 42 percent at Chicago; Carleton again stands alone, at 85 percent." In summing up, Brennan writes: "Clotfelter's data strongly suggest the presence of cross-subsidy from undergraduate to graduate education in part on the backs of undergraduates, who pay for it through large classes and limited access to senior faculty." And Brennan is no Ralph Nader; he is Dean of the University of Virginia's Curry School of Education.

As Clotfelter and Brennan show us, we thrust the tender young talent of this nation and much of our money into a system that only tangentially regards the education of eighteen- to twenty-two-year-olds as its primary goal. But at what cost? Are these universities providing our kids with a quality educational product, which will equip them for the twentieth century, or are they just our era's edition of the gas-guzzling behemoths of yesteryear?

3

HUNTERS OR THE HUNTED?

The future belongs to small, fast-moving, short-lived
adhocracies . . . digitized hunter-gatherer groups roaming the
steppes of cyberspace.
—*John Perry Barlow*

As a history teacher and college counselor working to help high school students prepare themselves for the rest of their lives, I find these words by John Perry Barlow, futurist pioneer, chilling. Because no matter how electronically hip these kids are, no matter how plugged-in, computer-literate, even digitized (whatever that means), when it comes to school, I too often see kids grazing through the semesters of their education, dutifully munching on whatever fodder schools toss to them as they docilely wait to be shipped on. They do this, of course, in hopes that the system has their lives all worked out for them if they stay within institutional fence lines. But reading words like Barlow's, I fear that when those fast-moving adhocracies show up on the horizon, it's the kids I work with who will be the ones hunted and gathered.

If this picture seems exaggerated, even apocryphal, let me share an anecdote from more than a decade ago, which still represents current attitudes. On what seemed like a regular enough teaching day, I walked into my class in Modern European History and, after a few preliminaries, began asking questions as usual. Soon, however, it became apparent that the group of tenth-grade scholars ranged before me seemed sheepish and fidgety, possibly because they didn't know a thing about the causes of the Franco-Prussian War, the subject under discussion. They were oddly quiet, as if they were attempting a feat of collective invisibility before my eyes. Naturally, I asked them what was up, and they informed me that an anomaly in the school calendar meant that grades were already set for the current marking period and nothing we did in class that day could be counted against them—so they had skipped the homework. Reminders like this about the power grades have over students are generally discouraging to teachers who hope for more in the way of intellectual engagement, but rather than dwell on that issue right then, I plunged ahead with other questions.

What, I asked, did they think a "bad" grade would actually do to them? Answering in near unison, they said a bad grade would mean they wouldn't get into a "good" college. And what would happen then? That would mean they wouldn't get into the "right" graduate school and hence the "right" firm or whatever and they might miss the "good" life altogether. It was a remarkable performance, and it seemed so obvious to them that work done in school should earn a coin specifically applicable in the future marketplace of their lives. Rather than regarding education as something that honed their thinking skills or taught them that learning to ask the right question might be more valuable than getting the right answer, these students viewed education exclusively as a paying proposition. With little coaxing from me, they had chanted out with stunning precision a collective vision of their futures. It sounded like a mantra, an orthodoxy they lived their lives around. If history was to be read, chemistry quizzes readied for, or an English essay written, it would be done with this theology in mind.

This discussion happened in the winter of 1983. Ronald Reagan was President and Gary Hart, not yet pictured aboard *Monkey Business* with Donna Rice on his lap, was viewed as the Democratic Party's leading intellect and presidential front-runner. I remember the chronology, because then I went to the board and wrote: EUREKA and BETHANY NAZARENE. When I asked what these words meant, everyone shook their heads, so I explained that Eureka was where President Reagan went to college and that Bethany Nazarene was Gary Hart's alma mater. If what you're interested in is fame and power from a college, these are proven winners. While I was saying this, I noticed the kids squirm in the face of these no-name colleges. I still remember the spirited fight they put up, how much faith they had in the system's power to dole out guaranteed rewards, how they scoffed at my attempts to get them to recognize a more existential view of education's potential benefits and teased me about being a naïve schoolteacher, clueless about the real world. As a class, it was an interesting exercise, but it left me, and still leaves me, feeling wistful that such bright, energetic students felt so locked in the grip of external institutions, were so preoccupied not by what they would do with their lives but by what, in their lives, would be done to them.

In our era's morality play, the scriptures have it thus. In the school-to-college pilgrimage, good (diligence, hard work, excellence) is rewarded with grades and "offices," and evil (sloth, incompetence, and so on) is punished by bad test scores and deselection, until an "elect" emerges from the sorting chutes to go off to the "right" colleges and after that, of course, to the "good" life, which as far as I could deduce from what my students said, is little more than possessing plenty of consumer options.

As a largely secular culture residing in suburban grids and shopping at malls that might as well have been lowered by helicopter, we are attempting the novel experiment of living lives bare of traditional anthropological scaffolding. Uncoupled from village life and often independent of multigenerational families, we find few legends and stories to guide us except those learned in school. For all of our seeming worldliness, this lack of cultural warp and woof in our lives renders us naïve. We jump at quick explanations and simple fixes. You could almost say the college pecking order that we hold sacred is based on an old-boy system, which was created during the heyday of industrialism when a handful of white males were divvying up the fruits of a virgin continent.

Do we really think this will adequately serve our children in a complex, global, postindustrial economy of the future? Yet instead of demanding that students develop their own life vision—their own medicine bundle of specific skills, curiosities, spiritual grounding, and entrepreneurial energy— we are fixated on college names, and in the frantic pursuit of this panacea we believe all manner of rumors about the process of college selection. No story about gilt-edged colleges snapping up oboe players, wide receivers, and Cherokee Indians (rather than our earnest and deserving children) seems too outlandish. These rumors, and the sense of panic they engender, lead us to spend great sums of money on score-boosting potions, or on private counselors as intermediaries in the hope of gaining special deals with higher powers, even though we know that by doing this we risk snatching the initiative out of our children's hands. When we spend money on these potions, we are arguably as gullible as illiterate medieval peasants conned by papal hucksters peddling indulgences guaranteeing entrance to heaven. But the families of college-bound children feel neither gullible nor naïve; they truly believe in the sanctity of this system to turn high school kids into winner adults by the single expedient of "name" colleges.

In fairness it should be stated that there are many meritocratic aspects to college admissions, and prestigious colleges do have strong student bodies, powerful faculties, and luxurious resources. Furthermore, there is nothing wrong with teaching children that there are systems in life based on hard work, ordered schooling, and deferred gratification. But given the value of our traditional college system, let's broaden the paradigm for a moment.

Intuitively, we hope that success in the world is built not so much around external admissions formulas as around internalized concepts, such as mindfulness, integrity, initiative, curiosity, self-direction, flexibility, and resilience. We hope that these concepts are best nurtured in young people who see the world around them as a multivariate puzzle to be tinkered with over a lifetime, not just as a series of hoops to jump through or drills to be endured.

Today, in their rush to cede control to institutions, many in the middle class—parents and children—seem to regard the teenage years as little more than a résumé-building sub-station. It's gotten so that even interscholastic athletics are seen mainly as tickets to a "better" college. Take, for example, the student who told me that he wished he hadn't played soccer after all because it wasn't doing him any good in college admissions.

"What do you mean?" I asked. "Didn't you have fun? Wasn't it worth it to play on those teams, to just kick the ball around?"

"Not if it doesn't help me get in," he grunted. Then he pulled his baseball cap down across his eyes in a discouraged manner, as if the system—which had apparently promised him more from soccer than the simple joy of playing hard at a game he was good at—had betrayed him.

Where, I wondered, is the spirit of "Just Do It" that Nike holds up in its ads with such eloquence?

This attitude certainly wasn't in evidence in one of my other students when I asked her, in passing, what she planned for the summer. Next week, she said, she was heading off for a bike trip in France. Then she made a funny face. When I asked what the face meant, she answered that she was making the trip not because she especially wanted to see the French countryside from the seat of a bicycle but because she thought that she might get a good college essay out of it. Of course, what she didn't know was that French bike trips had become such a cliché that her essay would most likely look like thousands of others, especially if its culminating moment described her speaking French to a lady on some park bench followed by the realization that language study brings people together. How could she know that when admissions officers see a bike-trip-in-France essay they head for the office coffee machine to help get them through it?

These stories about the state of over-organized, externally directed youth might be discouraging, but they can also inform us. They can help us realize that if kids set out on their own self-generated, self-directed pathways, not only will they achieve the fulfillment that comes with such independence, but they will get noticed as being very different from the résumé-obsessed herd moving down more well-worn trails. I think we would all agree that an essay based on a local pathway, explored with originality and depth of feeling, could be more compelling than one based on the French-bike-trip formula, and it is these explorations that should be encouraged.

There are risks involved in any independent course of action, certainly, but if that path is thoughtfully taken, the rewards outweigh the risks. Lately, I heard from a former student who, instead of going off to college after high school, had spent a year working on organic farms in New Zealand. He talked about the work, the travel, and the new sense of the world he had gained. There is little doubt that his freshman year is bound to be a richer, more potent undertaking because of the initiative he took. And students don't have to travel to Australia, either.

One of the best essays I ever read was by a young man who had spent several summers as an apprentice carpenter. His parents were the classic white-collar professionals about whom lightbulb-changing jokes are told. (Two. One to mix the martinis while the other calls the electrician.) He was certainly green when he came to the job. But his writing was filled with such lively specifics, about how hard it is to learn to work with hands and brain simultaneously, that by the end of the essay the reader could almost smell the pungent resin in fresh-cut pine and hear the twisting whine of power saws running too close to fingers. Finally, as his co-workers stopped teasing him and began to trust his measurements, we share his deeply felt triumph.

arc

Another dividend of our children setting out on their own pathways is that they won't be so vulnerable to the external judgments of teachers, coaches, counselors, etc., which often pulverize self-esteem. This is not to advocate the Lake Wobegone-ization of children and to claim that they are all above average. What it means is that we must help kids find ways to measure their self-worth that are more independent of institutional judgments. This is especially important because the decisions of admissions officers are often distorted by their own institutional imperatives. With football squads to field, alumni to placate, affirmative-action goals to meet, and development cases to coddle, the merits of individuals can be lost in the shuffle. Kids who have developed their own intellectual agendas will be less likely to let college admissions officers tell them who they are. Through their own initiatives, they will already have discovered that for themselves.

horse riding?

There is a well-known group exercise that asks participants to recall their most important learning experience. In a majority of cases, as it turns out, these learning experiences didn't happen in school settings. This is a crucial clue. It should help us to be more creative in the way we seek out and take advantage of learning moments for kids. Apprenticeships, enrolling in college courses while still in high school, independent study, reading for its own sake, community service, journal keeping, outdoor challenges, year-abroad programs, work that stresses process over product, taking time out between high school and college, or just making time to get to know an older person all become exciting options.

Students, with the help of their families, can seize control of their lives and reap powerful by-products as competent emerging adults (the first of which might be to make them into more effective college applicants). Our kids can step away from institutionally sanctioned sorting chutes and begin to chart their own courses. All it takes is the faith that initiative and responsibility are powerful, self-honed tools. And if we think about it, aren't these some of the very qualities we want our children to end up with anyway, especially as they square off to face those fast-moving adhocracies, riding low and hell-bent-for-leather just over the horizon?

A PARENT'S STARTER KIT: A DOZEN THINGS PARENTS CAN DO EARLY, VERY EARLY
(Arranged chronologically)

1. Read to your children whenever possible.
2. Turn the TV off.
3. Collaborate on meal preparation. Then, instead of grazing, sit down and talk while you eat.
4. Volunteer together somewhere, such as a food pantry or a homeless shelter.
5. Help kids build relationships with older people.
6. Resist shopping as an avocational/recreational activity.

7. Beware of time-intensive athletic programs that keep everyone busy on the only days available for family adventure.

8. Find ways to relate to the place where you live. Make its history and environmental health the family's business.

9. Take nonacademic process-oriented courses with your kids (e.g., woodworking, welding, pottery, Thai cooking).

10. Help kids find valid apprenticeships, where real skills are on the line, rather than letting them take mall jobs that risk addicting them to consumption.

11. Travel without itineraries. "Show up and be open" should be the motto of weekend trips.

12. Talk about goals; discuss building an education as if it were a piece of architecture going together brick by brick rather than a monolith that just appears at the end of school.

4

THE MIRACLE OF SCARCITY

A question I get asked all the time is "With the cost of tuitions going up and the number of families who can pay them going down, why is it still so hard for kids to get into colleges?"

I hate this question because my answer sounds so pretentious, like one of those irritating riddles handed down by guys who live in caves. Nevertheless, I go ahead and answer: "It's hard for kids to get into colleges because they only want to get into colleges that are hard to get into." Now you could sit on a cushion for a couple of days to think about what this means, or I could tell a few stories.

Several years ago, when I was doing college counseling at a high school in New York, I was talking with a very bright and capable junior who said she was interested in attending college in California. We talked about going out West to study and about how East Coast kids worked out the problem of distance and so on. Then we put together a list of schools, which began with Stanford, Berkeley, and UCLA. I also mentioned a smaller school named Pomona, one of the Claremont Colleges. When I did this, I noticed the slightest trace of disappointment cross her face, no more than a twitch really, but enough to notice. Our conversation continued a while longer, then the bell sounded for the next class (as it always does in high school), and I could tell, as she left the office, that she felt diminished. Accordingly, I wasn't all that surprised to get a call from her father later the same afternoon. But I was surprised that he was so agitated.

"Did you know," he asked, "that Stephanie is a very good student, in fact one of the best in your school?"

"Yes," I said, "I did know that."

"Well, when she talked to you, she didn't feel that way," he continued. "She felt like you didn't know a thing about her. She felt like you hadn't even read her transcript before she came in to talk to you."

"Wow!" I was thinking to myself as he spoke. "What did I do to stir this up?"

Then it occurred to me that it was the word "Pomona." Maybe he hadn't heard of this college. Maybe he didn't know it was one of the most selective colleges in the country. His daughter probably didn't either and had called him, upset that the only thing her hard work and achievement was going to get her was some booby-prize college. He was feeling the same way, and like a jerk to boot. He had spent big money for a private school, and when his daughter had gone in to find out what they were going to get for their investment, she came out of the counselor's office with some college she'd never heard of. Pomona. It sounded like a cleaning product to him.

Luckily, I had bought one of those big, tilt-back, swivel chairs precisely for moments like this, moments that called for a lot of listening. So I leaned back and gently swiveled, hearing him out, until his tirade showed signs of wearing down.

Only then did I venture a few words. I had to show him that I understood how he felt. I did, and I do. These days it is universally believed that education is a commodity. He had put up the hard cash, Stephanie had put up the equally precious coin of conscientious work and brainpower. They wanted something good for this "money." When I could show him admissions statistics that proved Pomona was very hard to get into, I could hear him relax. They were getting something for their money after all. That college with the funny name wasn't a family insult. He didn't feel foolish anymore.

Here is another story:

It's spring, and I keep noticing Joey hovering around, wanting to talk to me. I hadn't seen much of him, at least in an official sort of way, since he had been accepted to Duke as an Early Decision candidate in the fall. Joey is a top kid at school, smart in the classroom, a leader whose quick grin and knack for poking fun at himself makes him beloved in the community. He could have gotten into lots of places, but he chose Duke because he is a big Blue Devils basketball fan, and because he loves golf and thinks it would be great to attend a school where he can play the game year-round.

When he was admitted early to Duke, he was ecstatic—even though his friends thought he could do better.

But now he is lingering in the halls in a definitely non-Joey way, and I'm not sure what the edgy hovering is about. For all I know, his golf game is off. Anyway, I invite him into the office to catch up, and it doesn't take very long to get at what's bothering him.

"Sure, I'm still excited about Duke," he says. "Especially since it looks like Nelson is going down there, too."

"Whoops!" I think. "Here it is."

Nelson is famous in the senior class for shaving life close, for being sick on the days assignments are due, for buying term papers at local colleges, for almost flunking French because the new teacher thought he should know the subjunctive and not just talk about his travels in France during class. But Nelson is especially famous as the son of a software entrepreneur whose big new office complex is being built in the Research Triangle, adjacent to the Duke campus.

"At least when kids get to know us, nobody's going to think I went to some nerdy high school where kids just studied all the time," Joey said. "They'll think I'm a real goodtimer. Who knows, it might do wonders for my social life."

And then he grins at me. But the grin has too much irony to it, even a glint of bitterness. Right then I know that Joey has a case of the old I-used-to-think-the-college-I-got-into-was-fine-until-Tom-or-Dick-or-Harry-or-whoever-got-in-there-too blues.

And another story:

I'm talking to a parent named Richard. Over the past year it's been easy to admire him because he loves his kids so much and is so forthright about wanting the world for them. But over and over again he keeps asking me why I think his daughter is going to have a tough time getting into the college she wants to attend. I have already suggested other, less competitive colleges for them to consider. But neither father nor daughter can find any enthusiasm for the ones I mention, though they know these are fine schools and have even enjoyed visits to the campuses.

To help him understand, I decide on another tack. Richard is a talented businessman who drives a Range Rover and specializes in buying troubled companies, fixing them up, and selling them for a big profit. When it comes to a concept like supply and demand, Richard is not a newcomer. I also know him to be a very honest person, sometimes painfully so.

I ask him, just as an exercise, to think of selective colleges as businesses that have stumbled onto a magic formula that allows them to keep demand for their product growing steadily for decades. This magic formula is so good (it has worked in fat economic times and lean) and so powerful that it has enabled these colleges to raise their tuition prices over the years by an average of nine percent per annum, twice the increase of the consumer price index. And all these selective colleges have to do to maintain this magic power is to make sure they keep on rejecting lots of good kids every year. If they can keep rejecting good ones, the magic will go on forever. It's like the secret mine the Lone Ranger could go to for silver for his bullets any time he needed it. The only difference is that these colleges go to the mine and get more students to apply. Each time they do it, an increase in applications keeps places at their colleges scarce, which makes people want these places more.

What the colleges have done is take scarcity to a higher level, a level even above money.

Luckily, Richard knows me well enough to see the twinkle in my eye. At least I hope he does, so I go on.

"Think of it as something like the time you went down to buy your Range Rover. You plunked $50,000 on the counter, but instead of just picking up the check, the salesman said that he wanted you to fill out an application so the Range Rover people could see if you qualified to own one. Of course, you'd be outraged. But then this salesman was able to show you that only fifteen percent of the people who wanted to buy Range Rovers, and could afford them, actually 'qualified.' That's why they had the application."

Then I asked him, "If that happened and you qualified—were actually allowed to own one of their cars—would you pay even more? Do you think you might pay twice as much to be in such an exclusive club?"

Richard looked at me and thought for a minute. Then he smiled and said, "Yes, in that situation, if that's the way it really was, I'd pay the extra fifty grand."

You might think I made this up. But I didn't. It shows how bewitched we are by the things we might not be able to have.

5

MANUFACTURING SCARCITY

The stories I have shared thus far show that scarcity is on a lot of people's minds when they think about colleges. Accordingly, it didn't take savvy college administrators long to grasp that high application numbers in juxtaposition to low admission percentages were the key to a college being regarded as one of the "best." The history of a given college—its large endowment, winning athletic teams, snazzy location, fine campus architecture, great teaching faculty, and even proximity to skiing—might *contribute* to desirability; but none of these factors, not even a bunch of them in combination, would hold a candle in the public's mind to just plain hard-to-get-in-ness as a gauge of quality.

A brief, recent history of Brown University admissions

underscores this point. Brown, without question, has always been a fine school, but in terms of selectivity it was always a step or two behind the leaders. By the early 1950s, in fact, Brown resided at the bottom of the first tier of great universities. Maybe it was even in the second tier. Then a couple of things happened. The first was the formation of a football league by Harvard, Princeton, Yale, Dartmouth, and several other colleges, including the University of Pennsylvania, Columbia, and Cornell. The idea of the league's founders was the creation of a conference that would represent and enforce the high academic standards these schools had for student athletes. They wanted it as the basis of a football schedule. But this group consisted of only seven schools, and when it comes to forming a league in a sport that plays all its games on Saturday, even numbers work better. The problem was, which college should become the eighth? The college presidents and directors of athletics met hard and long on the subject and, at last, came down to two finalists: Colgate and Brown. Athletically, the two schools were hard to separate, especially since they had a long tradition of playing each other in a Thanksgiving Day football game. To choose one and not the other was a little like dividing Siamese twins. But divide this august group surely did, and Brown received the invitation, quite possibly because it was geographically closer to most of the other schools in the new conference.

Previous to this, the term Ivy League had been informally bestowed on certain colleges by journalists, sports fans, and songwriters, but there had been no official Ivy League until they put together that football schedule. As soon as Brown became a full-fledged member of this exclusive club, the Thanksgiving Day football game with Colgate was slated for oblivion and dropped from the list of ancient football rivalries.

In spite of this upward mobility via football schedule, Brown continued to languish in the selectivity doldrums, at least in relation to its Ivy League rivals, and was universally known, even to *The New York Times,* as the "doormat of the Ivy League." Because of this, throughout the late '50s and early '60s few high school students with an acceptance to another Ivy League college in hand (with the possible exception of Penn) ever chose Brown.

By the late 1960s, however, all of this had changed. Brown had become a "hot" college, in fact the very college for whom the label "hot" was originally created. How Brown managed this unprecedented changing of places can be traced not to any serious alteration in Brown's financial or faculty situation, but to a late 1960s educational restructuring and the arrival of a man named James Rogers as the university's director of admissions.

As a teacher who began his career at Manhattan's exclusive and academically demanding Collegiate School, Rogers, a Brown graduate, was well aware of the fashion dynamics surrounding college choice, and after receiving a master's degree from the Harvard School of Education in 1965, he decided that a stint in the Brown admissions office would be interesting, if only because it would give him an overview of secondary-school education. To say that things turned out to be interesting for him would be quite an understatement, especially after July of 1969, when he took over the post of director of admissions. As many of us will remember, the late '60s were notable for political and cultural ferment, especially on college campuses. Perhaps less memorable is the fact that Brown responded to the demands of its students for a "relevant curriculum" with a new way of viewing undergraduate education that turned out to be as radical as it was bold.

What happened was that two undergraduates, Eliot Maxwell and Ira Magaziner (who more recently became notable for his work on President Clinton's health plan), created what became known as the Maxwell-Magaziner Plan. Consistent with the ideology of the times, the plan put students at the controls of their own education by totally eliminating all core curriculum and major requirements. Henceforth, to graduate, a Brown student needed only to complete a certain number of courses; it didn't matter what these courses actually were. The philosophy of a core curriculum, with its innate subservience to the writings of dead white males, became a thing of the past at Brown. No longer would the university steer undergraduates, via a curriculum-wide set of requirements, into a variety of departments for the sake of educational breadth. Under the Maxwell-Magaziner Plan, if a student wanted to concentrate exclusively on courses in entomology or Russian poetry, what business was it to an "over-thirty generation" of academics and administrators? And anyway, weren't these the same people (at least in the widely held student view of the time) who not only had conspired in the corrupt society that had been forced down the throats of young people but had been architects of that biggest of all crimes: the war in Vietnam?

And if these changes weren't enough, the Maxwell-Magaziner Plan went even further. In order to promote risk-taking by students, the grading system at Brown was made student-friendly in the extreme. Not only were credit/no credit options extended to all courses, but a student electing to take a course for a grade could, if things were not going well, switch to a nongraded option at the last possible moment, leaving no paper trail for parents, graduate schools, or future employers ever to see. The rationale for this change was that it would help students dare to take courses outside their realm of expertise. Now engineers would take a chance on studying poetry and poets could risk taking science. Empowered by this new flexibility, Brown students would no longer be held hostage by the antiquated, elitist notions of their professors, and would at last be able to forge their own educational destinies.

Clearly, there was a good deal to recommend such changes, but in terms of admissions, the Maxwell-Magaziner Plan could have created a real mess. Consumers, already skeptical of Brown's doormat status, could have regarded this open-ended and potentially chaotic restructuring as evidence that the inmates had finally taken over the institution. If this perception had ruled, applicants might have stayed away in droves. But over in the admissions office, James Rogers had a different view. Instead of seeing the new program as a weakness, he would use it to revise the calculus of university admissions completely. He told me that "If you can differentiate yourself in a positive way [from the competition], it has to be an advantage." And then he chuckled and added, "There's a marketing principle in there somewhere."

Because the university's academic program was new, in Rogers's view, the Brown admissions office would think anew. Instead of seeking run-of-the-mill academic paragons, Brown would be looking for applicants who possessed special qualities of intellectual and emotional independence; the sort of young people who could best take advantage of the opportunities and flexibilities afforded by the new curriculum at Brown. Henceforth, being good at high school would no longer be good enough to get in, because too often these sterling students had sold out to traditional rituals and formulations. They wouldn't have the stuff to bob and weave to the rhythms of their own inner direction. To Rogers's way of seeing things, grinds and grade-grubbers of the Young Republican stripe who envisaged futures in "establishment" careers such as law and finance were not what his office would be after. "Reptilian," he called them. From now on Brown "admits" would be "with it" kids, socially and politically aware—"bellwethers," in his phrase, "who would have a following later on"—a new breed for a new age.

In order to attract plenty of these bellwethers, as well as screen out their reptilian antitheses, he hired recent graduates to staff his office—young people especially hip to the Brown scene. Always au courant with the latest attitudes, political fashions, and personal styles, these staffers did a wonderful job of attracting lively and interesting kids to Brown, and throughout the early '70s, the university's student body became widely known for its initiative and activism. These Young Turks of the admissions office were even more effective in deselecting other students. With uncanny X-ray vision, the young staffers could spot (or at least presumed they could spot) an incipient crypto-banker through even the thickest veils of early '70s fashion. And if they thought they detected what might later materialize into wing-tip shoes poking out beneath a pair of bell-bottom trousers, their verdict was rejection, no matter what sort of academic record the wearer might be packing.

Suddenly, and this was really astounding, some of the most powerful high school students in the nation, students who had hitherto regarded Brown as little more than a "safety school," got rejection letters in the mail.

Tremors of disbelief rocked the marketplace. Up and down the northeast corridor stories of suprising turn-downs shot across the circuit boards of the upper middle class with startling velocity. No suburban car pool or Episcopalian coffee hour was immune from tales of the Hotchkiss valedictorian who got the axe from Brown one day and got into Princeton the next, or the Scarsdale High School debating champion who was accepted to Harvard but not to Brown.

I remember that moment well. As a young college counselor at the Hackley School in Westchester County, New York, I often visited the admissions offices of colleges during the late winter in hopes of helping them better understand the strengths of the school I worked for and, in particular, the current year's applicant crop. The Brown office—located in haute Providence, in the old Corliss mansion with its high Victorian ceilings, huge walnut doors, and baroque plumbing facilities—was always a treat to visit. But I will never forget the year of the big switcheroo.

Just over thirty at the time, I was seated in a big chair, balancing a cup of coffee and a stack of folders with the records of my school's applicants. Across from me sat an even younger woman with her own stack of folders, knitting her brow and shuffling through the pile. In retrospect, I guess all that shuffling was an attempt to soften the news that Brown wasn't going to be able to take the top seven students in the class, even though their grades and SAT scores put them snugly at the top of Brown's published profile. Brown would, however, be able to accept Timothy, who, in spite of his rank near the bottom of the third decile and his spiky testing pattern, had written an essay that several staffers found interesting. Mind you, I had this pile of folders in my lap as well as the coffee cup, and I was sitting in one of those chairs that make your pants want to ride up too high. These discomforts certainly intensified the feeling that my young professional career was passing before my eyes. How on earth could I go back to my students and my boss and all those teachers and families with the news that our "best" kids weren't going to get into Brown this year, but a guy who was known for hanging out in the hallway playing the guitar would? To me, teetering in my chair, it seemed like the world was about to go upside down.

But then nearly as quickly, the whole world regained its balance. The explanation was simple—*Brown was "getting better."* So naturally it was becoming harder to get into. How else could one explain the rejection of those great students? How else could one explain the shifting of tectonic plates in the very bedrock of higher-educational status and prestige that turned Brown into the very first "hot" college?

And "hot" Brown clearly was. In a mere admissions season or two it skated right by Penn, Columbia, Cornell, Dartmouth, and even started taking kids away from the fabled Harvard-Yale-Princeton triad at the top of the Ivy pyramid. In fact, things got so good for Brown that James Rogers was able to make an even more daring move on the admissions chessboard.

For several years, Ivy League admissions deans (along with those from MIT) had been meeting in what was called the Ivy Admissions Group, whose mission it was to "adopt like procedures." One thing that concerned them was differences concerning early applications. For a decade or so, certain non-Ivy colleges such as Amherst and Williams had offered what they called "Early Decision," i.e. binding offers of admission to a handful of elite students who applied early and would, in turn, commit to attend the college if accepted. (In some measure, it was Amherst Dean Eugene Wilson's way of scooping up some of the best high school students in the country by getting them to commit to Amherst as they toured New England. With Early Decision, he could say to a young man he liked in an interview: "If you apply early to Amherst, we'll be able to take you in December." For kids on their way to interviews in Cambridge or New Haven the next day, such an offer from Wilson or his successor, Ed Wall, often proved irresistible, and the option helped Amherst hold its place in the ranks of America's most desirable colleges.)

In order to counteract preemptive strikes from Amherst and other top colleges, the Ivy Group tried to launch its own Early Decision plan but had trouble getting its members to agree on exactly what to do. On the one hand, Harvard—thinking that when all was said and done it had a shot at anyone it wanted—refused to back a plan that "bound" students to a college early. The University of Pennsylvania, on the other hand, refused to join any plan that *didn't* bind students to a college that accepted them early. Faced with this impasse, two plans developed. One group would continue with a traditional Early Decision plan; another group elected what they called an Early Action program, in which they would decide on early applications but would not obligate accepted students to commit until the regular May 1st candidates' reply deadline.

When this was proposed in an Ivy Admissions Group meeting, James Rogers remembers looking around the table to see who would opt for which plan, and when the positions became clear, he thought to himself that he could join with Penn, Cornell, Dartmouth, and Columbia in going with Early Decision, or he could join the ranks of Harvard, Princeton, and Yale and try Early Action. To him it was a no-brainer, but to much of the rest of the world a plan that allowed top-flight students to walk around with an early acceptance in hand, without ultimately being obliged to enroll, looked like a gutsy and brilliant move for Rogers and the Brown admissions staff. But probably no one dreamed what a difference it would make for Brown.

As Rogers had anticipated, it indeed locked Brown into the same paragraph with Harvard, Princeton, and Yale—right at the top of the heap. But even more importantly, it enabled Brown to showcase its burgeoning selectivity throughout the critical December holiday season when the parental rumor mill was operating full tilt. From the office Christmas party right through the Super Bowl, people with drinks in their hands could talk about which first-rate students had been "deferred" this year by Brown. And with every deferral Brown was able to make, its scarcity quotient edged up a point or two, its hotness grew hotter, guaranteeing that the following year there would be even more Early Action candidates to repeat and intensify the process.

6

SEPARATION ANXIETY

TRY NOT TO JUDGE
A COLLEGE BY YOUR FEELINGS OF LOSS

As kids set off on the pathway to higher education, often toward some distant place and usually in what seems like alien surroundings, it is clear that college admissions is about beginnings. But it is also about endings. Families change when children leave for college. Suddenly there are empty and quiet spaces that only moments before were bursting with color and sound. Suddenly the phone stops ringing so much (except for those odd-hours calls from the dorm) and doors quit their irritating, wonderful slamming. We notice changes everywhere, even in a piece of leftover roast chicken that hangs on forever in the refrigerator. We might kid ourselves into thinking the peace is worth the respite it provides from late-night vigils that kept us listening for the thunk of a car door in the driveway, signaling that everything was safe at last, and there might be a younger sibling in the family who cheers the departure of his older brother because it means the possibility of a bedroom upgrade. But for most of us, when a member of the family leaves for college, it's a painful, empty time which can catch us off guard.

Here is a phone call I remember getting from Randy's father. It's January of the boy's senior year. The father wants to go over Randy's list of colleges with me one more time, just to be sure we have it right, so we start at the top with what we both agree are a couple of "unlikelies," work our way through a few "barely possibles," and finally get to a "probable." In this case it is Hobart. Randy's father's voice is tense on the phone. He gropes for words carefully, but this doesn't mask his anger and disappointment. We talk about Hobart, and I try to reassure him with specific cases of former students who have gone on to great college careers there—how much they grew, how much they valued the school later in their lives. I even recall one student who had barely left home before college but won a Watson Fellowship that funded a year's travel and research in Latin America after he graduated from Hobart. I suggest that Randy is primed for the same sort of growth. I also remind him that when Randy and he had visited the college the previous summer, he had reported it as a place that would work well for his son.

"Yeah," he said, "but it was just a theory then. Now it's real."

Something has clearly changed. It must be that the time

for Randy's leave-taking has drawn ever closer. And now, to this father, Hobart doesn't seem "good" enough to take his son away from him. If it were Harvard or Haverford or even Hamilton, he might be able to talk himself into believing the loss of his son would be worth it. But not Hobart.

Early in my career as a college counselor I would have regarded his nit-picking and disparagement of a fine college irritating. Now I understand how much it shows a father's pain.

"Boy," I say, "you're going to miss him, aren't you?"

"Oh goodness, yes," he answers, voice cracking. "I knew he was going, but I didn't know it would be this hard."

We talked for a while about kids leaving home, about a father's life without football games to cheer for or a boisterous bunch of kids barging into the kitchen afterward. We comforted ourselves with the usual jokes about how our kids will move back home after college anyway—and then really drive us crazy. By the end of our conversation he was feeling better, not because I had talked him out of the pain of his loss, but because he was able now to differentiate between his anxiety over college admissions and his pain over separation. The question of "who gets in where" had settled to its appropriate level.

College admissions will always, and properly, be regarded as one of life's important contests—like stretching for a new job or bidding on the house of our dreams. However, uncoupled from the distress of saying farewell to a child, the admissions contest itself looks more like a pothole on the road of life than a chasm families can't get around or over.

Interestingly, I've found that mothers aren't so often taken by surprise by the pain of a daughter or son leaving home. Perhaps women have a stronger intuitive sense of family wholeness, which helps them anticipate their loss. In fact, some women say their eyes have been filling up over the prospect of losing their kids for years. But like their male counterparts, these women are relieved to discover that their anxiety over college admissions is at least as much about separation as it is about specific outcomes. With this insight in place, parents can cut through the emotional clutter and start thinking more clearly about the process. For example, questions about a college's size and its distance from home don't seem as threatening. They find they can talk to their children more objectively about college options, really weighing the pros and cons, when they no longer have to find a campus situation perfect enough to warrant their loss.

But no matter how you slice it, when our kids leave home things change. Sometimes it seems as if it couldn't happen at a worse time. Dad is working on his midlife crisis, Mom is approaching menopause, and the family dog isn't feeling too well either. And now these kids of ours, who just got to be a little bit of help around the house and are becoming more and more fun to talk to, threaten to split to a West Coast college to the tune of a hundred and fifty thousand dollars. Luckily for us, certain things about their behavior ease the pain of their leaving town.

HOW OUR KIDS RESPOND TO LEAVING HOME: OR MAYBE THAT'S WHY HE'S DRIVING US SO CRAZY

"Clownage" is how a friend described his son's senior year behavior: cutting out of school before French class on some phony excuse of a doctor's appointment, or staying out too late and then demanding immunity from parental prose-cution on the grounds that next year no one will be telling him when to come home. If dirty clothes were against the law, his room would be shut down by state authorities, yet any attempt to mitigate the situation is met with claims of privacy. And that Barking Spiders album playing full blast all the time could be doing structural damage to the house. Yet in the next instant this same kid is an angel of aid and comfort. He even took his little brother bowling the other day. Just the two of them.

If you ask mental-health professionals what's going on here, they will tell you it's a dress rehearsal for leaving home. To ease the pain of departing for college, our chil-dren apparently need to make us hate them. Then, presum-ably, they can muster the energy to leave. Rehearsing separation is so universal it even occurs in boarding schools, where kids have to break the bonds of an institution that has become like a family to them. Every year, administrators report that some of their most dependable school citizens start acting crazy in the spring of senior year. Senior spring it is called, or senioritis or senior slump. A real virus. Seniors smoke on the fire escapes, drink in the basements, and play pranks, such as installing an offensive flag on the roof of the main building just before spring alumni weekend brings huge numbers of graduates back to campus. The motivation for all this clownage at home and at school is probably un-conscious, but that doesn't make it any easier for families or teachers to bear. The good news is that kids usually get over it before graduation, which means that some of the worst salvos of anti-institutional behavior are quickly fol-lowed by unnerving torrents of sentimentality in which the crankiest of teachers and the starchiest of regulations are elevated in kids' minds into institutional rites of passage: the very things that *made* high school for them. The home-front equivalent is that our children suddenly think they like us after all. Out of the blue they want to help with grocery shopping or cleaning the garage.

Another phenomenon is that, swept up in the fierce embrace of leaving home, many kids want to museumize their childhood. Favorite old-time menus are requested, and the velvet rope of tradition is readily invoked to prevent even the slightest alteration to their personal spaces. And later, in the fall or at Christmas, if they return home from college to find a little brother ensconced in their room or, worse yet, a parent using it for some worthy project, their response can seem out of scale with the amount of territory actually lost. But remember, this too is about the pain of separation.

In an era when we hear a lot about the decline and demise of the American family, it is surprising that so many kids take leaving home so hard. But we should remember that for all the changes that have washed over family life in the last three decades, in many instances life at home has more intimacy and informality than it did the generation before, when a lot of us had "ma'am" and "sir" relationships with our parents and in return were often spoken to as "young man" or "young woman." Most of us would agree that the pace of modern family life can be pretty crazy, but for all the passing-like-ships-in-the-night chaos, for all the refrigerator grazing and on-the-go laundry sorting that characterizes the contemporary domestic scene, there must be something about our families for kids to like—they seem to miss us so.

PART 2

AN OVERVIEW OF THE YEAR AHEAD

7

YOUR ADMISSIONS TIME LINE: ANNOTATED

SOPHOMORE YEAR

October: PSAT Until a few years ago, this first brush with the College Board happened in the eleventh grade. Then some marketing wizard at Princeton had the idea that they could double test revenue by offering the PSAT to high school sophomores. Many counselors were opposed to this on the grounds that it would get the standardized-test pot boiling a year earlier, that low scores would erode the self-esteem of tenth graders struggling to pull themselves out of the adolescent trough, and that the high-scoring underachiever would be able to say, "No sweat Mom, check out those scores," then sit back down to his video game. But these concerns were swept aside by a tide of people who convinced themselves that tenth-grade testing would be a good practice session. Many people say PSATs don't count for anything, and this is mostly true. The trouble is, PSAT scores correlate closely with SAT scores, and very few people say *they* don't count. So the score a child gets in the tenth grade can look mighty imposing, even if people do say it's just a practice deal. The best thing families can do at this stage is to stay calm and try to resist the impulse to call Kaplan or the Princeton Review for a full pre-PSAT overhaul. Use the tenth-grade test score as a baseline. Occasionally, it has even served as a useful wakeup call.

College Visits Visiting colleges at this early stage can seem like a good idea to parents who are curious about what lies ahead. These parents might, however, find considerable resistance to visits on the part of fifteen-year-olds, who equate "college" with the unsettling concepts of cut-throat competition and possible rejection. With this in mind, tenth-grade college tours should be casual drive-bys at speeds rarely lower than 25 mph. Special safaris to historically significant campuses with plants growing up the walls can intimidate kids whose main preoccupation is sitting with the cooler kids in the school cafeteria.

Spring Course Sign-ups for Junior Year Junior and senior year courses are the ones with the real impact on who gets in where. What you will hear from high school kids at this time of year is that it really doesn't matter what sort of courses you take, it's the grades that count. There is a grain of truth in this, and over the next year your admissions grapevine will probably report the success of some academic con artist who managed to slip into a hot college with good grades in lightweight courses. But mostly this talk is the equivalent of "all the other kids are going" and should be given about that much weight. The fact is that selective colleges make a big deal about a rigorous-looking transcript and hate to feel that they are getting fooled. This attitude explains some of the current enthusiasm for Advanced Placement (AP) courses. But kids shouldn't take AP courses just because they look good; success in challenging courses has the power to raise self-esteem at a critical juncture. Be sure to check out the whole range of good courses, not just the ones with the AP label. A locally created social studies course on, say, urban America might be a vigorous intellectual undertaking or it might be just a chance to listen to gangsta rap in the classroom. If it's a valuable course, a case for its vitality and importance can be made to colleges by the teacher (in the form of a recommendation), by the school's college counselor, or in an essay. In this way, art and music courses can also be validated to even the most conservative college. Sure, AP Chem sounds great, but if Johnny loathes chemistry there's a slim chance it's going to work out well. Needless to say, this course-choosing business is an area in which parents and kids should work together. And everyone should try to be honest. A parent fighting to turn a daughter into an engineer by coercing her into AP Physics is of no more use to these discussions than a kid trying to avoid a Shakespeare course on the sole grounds that it meets during first period. The idea is to create the right balance of courses, which have the appearance (and presumably the reality) of rigor without putting students in an impossible position *or* snuffing out mental engagement.

Summertime This post-ten-grade summer can be a tough one. Most kids are too young for real jobs or the drivers license and car to deliver them to it. At the same time, they are a bit too old to simply Nintendo their way through the dog days. Outdoor challenge courses sponsored by groups like Outward Bound or the National Outdoor Leadership School can be ideal here, as can unpaid apprenticeships or some sort of entrepreneurial venture doing yard work or providing child care at the neighborhood level. Try talking to parents and kids who have recently navigated this stage for their ideas. Maybe your brother-in-law needs his hedge transplanted and is willing to hire your kid.

JUNIOR YEAR

October: PSAT (Again) and NMSQT PSATs still don't "count," but now there is that NMSQT part. It stands for National Merit Scholarship Qualifying Test, which is sponsored by a separate corporation contracting with the College Board for scores on which to base awards. Over two million high school juniors take the test, and of these, fifteen thousand become semifinalists on their way (if subsequent testing and a brief scan of their transcripts corroborates their scores) to becoming finalists. Few National Merit Scholarships are actually awarded by the NMSQT Corporation; instead most are funded by individual colleges and businesses that have put up money.

September, October, November: College Reps at School This might be the time you find out you have a normal child. One evening, in a very off-hand way, your daughter allows that she met with the Princeton representative who was visiting her school. At this news, your instrument panel snaps onto full alert. *"Yes,"* you think, *"at last!"* Then she says, dipping her fingers in her cran-raz juice and drawing sticky designs all over the kitchen counter, "It really sucked!" You're stunned. Over the past year you've had random thoughts about places like Princeton, but "really sucks" wasn't one of them. Naturally, you ask what, in this particular instance, the phrase might mean. So she says that by the time she got to the meeting, all the industrial-strength pre-med weenies in the world were there, the "4.3 people," squeezed into the front rows with their notebooks gaping (these are her words). And of course they knew everything and had all sorts of questions about whether it was possible to do a bio-engineering–classical languages–eco-ethics triple major at Princeton. On top of this, she said, there were the "people who know people"—lanky field-hockey players with year-round tans whose fathers and grandfathers had gone there. *"And there wasn't anybody normal in the room,"* she cries out. Now she's twisting her hair into little braids, which the cran-raz juice is making stick straight out from her head like Pippi Longstocking's. That's when you begin thinking this college admissions business is going to be a little bit complicated after all. But that's also when you should know you have a normal daughter. God love her.

January, February, and March: Actually Getting Started These are the months when kids should begin exploring options. Remember, their first curiosities are tender shoots peeking out onto what seems to them to be a pretty scary world. At this point it's okay for you to take the initiative and buy a couple of college guides (I certainly hope you're not just *borrowing* this one), find out about computer access to college information, suggest a few campus drive-bys, and encourage kids to make an appointment with a college counselor at school. Don't get panicky when your suggestions are not acted upon that day, but don't let things slide indefinitely.

Conversations between parents and high school students on the subject of college admissions call for patience on everyone's part. Patience and activity. Tricky, isn't it?

Winter and Spring Vacation Visits For those tough enough to brave sleet, mud, and the flotsam and jetsam of campuses emerging from a long winter, this is not a bad time to look at a few schools. The trip might be grueling, but as far as New England, New York State, and the upper Midwest are concerned, the scene you'll see is closer to the real thing. Fall foliage might bloom all year long in the viewbooks, but ice and mud is the actual story. And besides, instead of being distracted by college cuties flinging frisbees around on the quadrangle, the family will be able, against the drab landscape of winter's end, to focus on what's really at stake in a college education.

January, March, May, or June: SAT This is it. But instead of discussing the full ins and outs of testing, here we simply mention the problem of getting a test-taker not only registered but physically (and, we hope, mentally) to the test site on time with a couple of number two pencils firmly in hand. The typical registration drama often begins months earlier at the high school, when the college office distributes College Board or American College Test booklets to the junior class. Of course they do this in a timely fashion—so timely, in fact, that our kids, known as they are for their ability to live in the moment, regard the deadline as something that probably won't happen in their lifetimes. So they stuff the booklets into the sub-basements of their lockers along with some scrunched-up math quizzes, a greasy San Jose Sharks hat, a few overdue library books, and a squashed Twinkie. Then they forget all about them. The result is that on the evening of the due date, all the registration stuff is composting away back at school while the check and the stamp and the last-minute, frenzied motivation to actually deal with the situation is at home. Luckily, a few panicky phone calls to friends reveal the existence of a late-registration option available for an extra fee. But once again, the date of this option is sufficiently far in the future to induce another episode of clerical amnesia. So everything is pushed to the "standby" option. This extra-cost service offered by the College Board (whose administrators must have teenagers of their own) involves the late fee plus a walk-in fee. But the worst part is not the money; it's the anxiety of not knowing whether or not there will be sufficient space at the test center to accommodate everyone in the standby predicament, which often means that standby kids approaching the test center will be doubly jittery.

May and June: SAT II, the Subject Tests These used to be called Achievement Tests. They are based on specific subjects. The Subject Test in Writing is required by many colleges. The most selective colleges require this test and two others. The same registration procedures and potential for sign-up and test-site-arrival chaos apply, although one hopes that a learning curve is beginning to show itself on the graph of family life.

Goals for a Spring Meeting with the College Counselor Find out how your school's college office moves the process. No matter what the format is (student-counselor, student-parent-counselor, parent-counselor), the idea is to get professional input about which colleges will be good matchups in terms of program and ambiance, and which ones are, admissions-wise, in the ballpark.

Sometime Later That Spring: Could Order Possibly Emerge from All This Chaos? It's been hard so far. The wondering and the false starts. But now a plan seems to be emerging in the list of colleges the family has in hand for summer visits. You even spot a few job applications going in to local businesses or hear talk about signing up for an enrichment course at a local college. But most encouraging of all is a new sense of engagement on the part of your child. It even seems that he or she will finish up strong on final exams.

Summer College Tour This can be the critical moment when kids take over the process from their parents. Often it happens on the road, or over the next month or so. It seems that somehow kids catch a glimpse of their future and the glimpse sticks. Dave sees himself approaching a college library, curious and resolved. Jody pictures herself bent over a microscope. Sam is stretching before practice, confident he can make the team. These are images in a crucial trajectory. Let's hope they begin to sink in and that the child who started the college visit trip in the back seat might take the wheel on the way home.

SENIOR YEAR

Back at School: Talks with the College Counselor Every year college counselors are amazed at how the kids they work with have grown since their first junior-year meeting. (In fact, a lot of us credit this maturity surge to our sagacious counsel.) When things are working right, high school seniors should be able to report to the counselor what they have seen on their visits as well as their inclinations for actual applications. This can be the foundation of an effective list. When things aren't working well, I suspect the culprit may be tension over money or someone's inflated expectations. If financial worries are at the forefront, I suggest you consult chapter 15, Money on Your Mind. As for high expectations, they call for honest assessment and communication between all parties. Family members should look into their motives carefully. For example, if someone is pushing a child to apply only to the "most competitive" colleges just to keep up with a brilliant cousin, now is the time to get real. Simply put, a slate of applications heading into the stratosphere can make senior year hell for everyone.

Early Fall: Closing In (The balance of responsibility has shifted to your child, so I spin the rest of this chronology in that direction. However, this doesn't mean that you can't keep right on reading.) The rumor mill at school and in the neighborhood is really grinding now. Everyone seems to have an edge except you. You've got test-prep pressure, so you're doing a cram course for three hours every Sunday morning. You've got résumé-padding pressure, so you try running for president of the stamp club without becoming a member. You toy with the idea of switching into AP Calculus, even though you know it would be suicide by slow equation. Early Decision madness is rampant at school and in the supermarket check-out line. Everyone in the cafeteria says if you don't get in early you don't get in at all, but you are clueless about where to take your Early Decision shot. Then there is the teacher recommendation scramble. Will Mr. Jones still hold a grudge about that term paper you handed in late last spring? Could your French teacher possibly do the job for you? You and your lame French accent? Counting on Mr. Smith, an all-purpose recommender of last resort, won't help either. Now everyone is saying he is too stupid to write a decent letter. Everyone is saying . . . Everyone is saying. . . .

Halloween: "Everything That Rises Must Converge"
Here's what happens in one week. The first quarter ends in a flurry of big tests and papers due, and the grades you get on these will determine whether you will be a brain surgeon or dumpster operator. (At least that's what everyone says.) The fall sports season ends in a barrage of do-or-die games. Early Decision deadlines close in. The leaves fall off the trees, the clocks are turned back (totally eliminating sunlight from your life), the flu season gets underway, and your chances of having the right date for the Halloween dance go from slim to nil. Luckily, on this stretch of bad road your parents are behaving perfectly: helpful but not intrusive, humorous but not grating, always ready to drive down to Federal Express to mail a late application without so much as an "I told you so."

Mid-December: Early Decision News Flashes For the Early Decision applicant, this season begins in the last days before vacation. It is a matter of endless waiting punctuated by jolts of news mixing the good, the bad, and the just plain ugly. Some kids are in and some kids aren't. Friendships shatter—at least for a minute or two. There's a great deal of running up and down the halls at school trying to get to the pay phone for word from home without making the call become a public event. There are shudders of community-wide disbelief: the valedictorian gets deferred; the son of somebody-or-other gets in. Several years ago, at a large, affluent New Jersey high school, a girl who had just been admitted to Harvard early was stopped in the hallway by a distraught classmate she didn't know. "Your father went there?" the questioner demanded to know. The girl nodded. "And your brother, too?" The girl answered, "Yes." "I thought so," the other hissed, turned on her heel, and disappeared down the corridor. This is the season parents call each other for news or call the school to vent their outrage. In these last few days at school before the holidays, the college office becomes a very lively spot as counselors help students struggle for perspective. Deferred kids are reminded of the options that still remain; accepted kids are counseled to be gentle with those who weren't; parents are reassured with contingency strategies. The clerical staff, breaststroking its way toward January 1st paperwork deadlines, will hopefully get a little eggnog, and the college counselors will (quietly and with great dignity) once again come down with the flu. Just in time for the holidays.

It is this crazed, overwrought moment in time that blows college admissions out of all proportion in the public mind. Across the nation's early winter landscape, an obsession with scarcity stirs our deepest fears and causes people to leap as one toward a formula, insisting that in this dog-eat-dog world, only College X will equal Job Y. At the exact moment when platters of Cajun blackened shrimp on toothpicks are offered at office parties the nation over, a scramble for the lifeboats is under way again.

Christmas Vacation: Application Time, Big-time Six, eight, ten, twelve of them. In this exercise, a flowchart is critical for monitoring what's done and what's still to do. Also, a large, flat work surface that is safe from cats and little sisters. Also, a big, fat piece of time. The "Common

Application" used by several hundred colleges helps; so do applications on disc or over the Internet. But still, it's an ordeal that takes family-wide understanding and support. Almost the only good thing about it is that you'll all feel better when it's over.

January: Financial Aid Forms and Remaining Applications The federal government insists on actual numbers from the end of the calendar year, so you can't send things in before January 1st (as if there was any great danger of that happening). But once New Year's has passed, get the forms in as soon as possible—because late filers often find the money is gone by the time they get organized. January is also the month when you wind up applications and make certain, at the gut level, that your slate of colleges is good. If your small inner voice keeps insisting that, safety-wise, you are not covered, this is the time to deal with it. Scrambling around in April for colleges with empty beds is no fun at all, and your chances of getting financial aid then aren't so great either.

February and Early March: Hibernation Time One reason to get things done right and in a timely fashion is to make the depths of winter bearable. You have given it your best shot and now, with your fate in the hands of others, this month becomes a needed hiatus between the craziness of application deadlines just passed and the high-anxiety weeks just over the horizon. So come down off the gerbil wheel you've been grinding away on for the past year: get to know your friends again, remember the simple pleasures of family life.

March and Early April: Getting the News By the middle of March, colleges begin sending out letters. The Rolling Admissions news usually comes first (from colleges making decisions and writing to candidates as they make decisions rather than waiting for a single mailing day). Mostly, the first news is good. It lays down a base of individual and collective confidence (and is reason enough to apply to a Rolling Admissions school or two). As this news comes in, the college admissions system seems to make sense at last. Kids have applied to colleges and they have been accepted. They begin to grow attached to places that have sent them good news. Dwell on this and avoid being distracted by what's to come.

April Need Not Be the Cruelest Month This is the moment you have been waiting for. No matter how much perspective any of us bring to such an event, it is hard to approach judgment day without a lump in the throat. So go gently into this one, win or lose, and above all try to think before you speak. On the chance that you're a winner, the folks next door or your friends at school may not be experiencing the same sort of triumph you are. And if things go badly for you, it will be better for everyone concerned to handle it at home for a while before taking your disappointment public. Of course, if your list of colleges was right to begin with, you should have some good choices as the mail rolls in. The key attitude here is not to think solely in terms of a hierarchy. Besides definitive answers, you may be placed on a waiting list, or two or five. Waiting lists are big these days. Because financial-aid awards are no longer fixed among a group of colleges, admissions officers can't predict as clearly where students in need of aid will choose to enroll. If you get put on a Wait List and you want to go to that college, you have to let its admissions office know of your interest. Let your counselor know what you want and write to the college. If you were accepted to every place you applied, feel good about what you have accomplished. Avoid thinking you should have shot higher. Enough already!

Late April: Choices Work hard at this one. It's important you feel that you have made the right selection. Remember, research shows that what you actually do in college is what matters. So find the place that will help you get smarter, more adept, better able to develop the qualities that you like most about yourself. This may not happen at the school with the nicest student center or where the kids have the coolest footwear. So look carefully—outside and in.

May: Don't Give Up on High School Even though every bone in your body tells you its time to blow off high school—that it's over—try to keep up academic appearances. If you do, you will find the faculty will go along with you, because the last thing anyone at the high school wants to do is give you an empty diploma case. And, in the long run, the last thing you want is to leave high school making the people you have worked with feel needlessly diminished.

June: Thank Your Parents for Everything They Have Done for You Then let them be proud of you.

PART 3

THE DISCOVERY PHASE: FINDING OUT
WHAT'S OUT THERE FOR YOU

8

THE TOOLS OF THE TRADE

One of the more bewildering aspects of the college admissions process is the mountain of information—books, videos, viewbooks, CD-ROM compendiums, and Web sites—that looms over families, threatening to sweep them away in an avalanche. But college is about information, and to access this information one needs tools. The trick is to move gingerly, to select carefully, and, always, to keep expectations moderate.

We college counselors suggest that somewhere in the middle of the junior year families equip themselves with a big college book. It makes parents feel better to have a resource like this around the house, and although their children may *not* say, "Gosh, Pop, thanks for going to all the trouble of buying a big college book, it looks like a swell resource," that doesn't mean they aren't grateful. As we have noted at other points, kids are naturally reluctant to embark on an enterprise like college admissions, which not only signals the end of childhood but also may involve them in a process of triage. It's a good time to keep in mind that for all their loud adolescent attitudes—many of which begin with "Oh Mom"—they will be sneaking peeks at the big book when you're not home. (And if it wasn't for those telltale potato-chip-grease stains on the pages, you might never know.) So parents should not wait for their children to take the lead in book procurement, just as students should be tolerant of parental attempts at getting going, even if they regard these as premature.

With this settled, the next question is what book (or books) should one buy? How you answer this question may gauge the level of obsession at which you are operating. (If, for instance, you find yourself buying one of each at Barnes and Noble and then need to go to Borders to see what they have, you may get a glimpse of the pressure you are putting on yourself and your child.)

In terms of big books, there are two categories: the narrative genera that provide breezy descriptions and subjective "ratings," and the more encyclopedic variety that are really compilations of lists. Both have their uses, and the type you choose may be a matter of personal style. If you want to know whether a student can major in hotel administration, minor in classics, play intercollegiate badminton, live in a fraternity house, keep a car on campus freshman year, and work in a radio station all at the same college (and, presumably, in the same lifetime), the encyclopedic variety may be for you. If, on the other hand, you are content to let distant editors interpret for you the relative levels of academic rigor on campuses or how much fun everybody (whoever that is) has on weekends, the more subjective variety can fill the bill—with the obvious caveat being that the opinions contained therein should be taken with quite a few grains of salt.

This doesn't mean the subjective reporting isn't true. What it means is that subjective opinions, to be credible, must purvey the most universally understood conventional wisdom regarding each college. If they don't, readers simply won't believe them. If you bought a book that said Dartmouth students employed the relative isolation of their Hanover, New Hampshire, campus to master a few extra physics formulas on Saturday nights, you'd be back at Borders to demand a refund before the Visa carbon had cooled. You'd feel duped, because no matter how hard its admissions office has tried to alter the conventional wisdom, most people think that on Saturday nights Dartmouth is a party sort of place, not a physics sort of place.

Because we cling to the road map of conventional wisdom so tightly, guides become powerful perpetuators of stereotypes, and these determine not only who will apply to certain schools but also, even more crucially, who among accepted candidates will ultimately choose to enroll. It's a case of a chicken-and-egg cycle that becomes self-fulfilling. If, for example, a strong-minded, intellectually lively feminist interested in studying physics wants to attend Dartmouth, she will have to run a gauntlet of self-appointed experts counseling her to do no such thing—even though Dartmouth has taken powerful steps over the past decade to make its science education for women superlative. Then if she ultimately decides to attend Dartmouth, unless she ends up winning a Nobel Prize in Physics, she will have to live with a lifetime of second guessing.

Another important, and perhaps more useful, aspect of college guides is that they present rough statistical parameters for who gets in by providing the average test scores of admitted applicants, class rank percentiles, and the like. Although, according to *The Wall Street Journal*, this data is occasionally stretched by colleges jockeying for position in the selectivity pecking order, the data is still useful for its predictive value in helping families create a slate of colleges that will ultimately yield a satisfactory group of acceptances. Other tools may be more effective for finding a good match between a student and a college, and the best place to start is with the material colleges send you for free: direct mail and videos.

VIEWBOOKS

It seems reasonable to suppose that interested kids can crack the college code by reading through the admissions materials, viewbooks, etc., that magically appear in the mail of virtually any household with a college-bound child. But in many instances disillusionment sets in with the first brochures that arrive. Kids, who hope a flood of direct mailings from Ivy League colleges will wrap the matter up before they're forced to give it serious thought, can be disappointed by those first couple of brochures from more prosaic colleges in the nation's center. And for the cynical, the first bits of mail can be hopelessly inappropriate: brochures from West Point sent to pacifists, auto-mechanic fliers sent to aspiring rocket scientists, that kind of thing. To hear kids tell it, if there was a meat science major, vegetarians would surely be getting full-color viewbooks.

Of course, what's really bugging these kids is that they have heard of so few of these colleges. This hurts their feelings. They can't help thinking that demographic deities in mail rooms high above have settled the question of what sort of college they will attend, so they quite naturally ignore any piece of mail with a college name on it, leaving parents to hover nervously about the growing piles and wonder if the fire inspector might raid the house.

HOW DIRECT MAIL WORKS

In most cases, college-bound students get mail because they have checked a release box on either their PSAT, SAT, or ACT registration materials indicating an interest in hearing from colleges that are hunting for students like them. Armed with these releases, the testing agency sells student names to colleges. But colleges do not buy random names, they buy the names of students who fit into specific profile groups, as determined by test scores and information students provide about themselves on test registration questionnaires. If kids fill out the questionnaires accurately, the potential for close matchups between college and student can actually be quite good. Over the past twenty years, many college admissions officers have effectively mastered the arcane science of direct-mail marketing, and if they can do their jobs, the results can be uncanny.

But surprisingly, admissions officers are not always left to do their jobs. The reason is that college faculties, boards of trustees, or college presidents often interfere. Although there are many possible variations to the form this interference takes, the following case will help you understand an archetype.

At Sandy River College (a fictional, but typical, liberal arts college), the faculty has decided, in its wisdom, that the kids at the college aren't smart enough, as demonstrated by their test scores. To remedy this, they want the admissions office to recruit students with higher numbers. This will enhance teachability, and, as test averages at Sandy River go up, a powerful halo effect will occur. The individual prestige of faculty members in their particular professional associations will also rise. Instantly, they will walk taller at national and international meetings as well as get their work published in various professional journals. This, in turn, will bolster their professorial rank at Sandy River, their marketability at upstream colleges, and, ultimately, their financial security.

One can well imagine the attraction an upward levering of test scores will have for faculty members. Suddenly the soporific drone of faculty meetings is punctuated by dramatic pronouncements. Masters in their own fields, professors are generally the type of people who assume that they can quickly master anyone's field, especially something as simple as admissions work. "Marketing," previously a dirty word to the leather-elbow-patch crowd, becomes their new religion. They want it and they want it fast. But instead of letting the admissions professionals use their best judgment to target students who have traditionally been interested in Sandy River, these self-appointed experts insist that the admissions office buy the names of students with higher scores, sometimes even the very highest scores. In speeches they say: "If you shoot for mediocre students, that's what you'll end up with. It's your job to shoot for the best, and then make them want to come to Sandy River."

It's just such talk that accounts for the tidal wave of brochures pouring through mail slots all over the nation. While these faculty dynamics may be hard on postal workers and trees, the good news is that your child needn't have his self-esteem lowered by anything that comes in the mail. These days it's too random to take personally.

Nevertheless, if you can muster enough sorting and filing stamina, interesting nuggets can be gleaned from mailings. All it takes is a little patience and a good filing system. So get yourself some hanging folders and a file box and, after a quick scan, save the brochures from schools that meet general parameters and specific program needs. If you do this, you will be startled by the smorgasbord of higher education possibilities that stretches out before you. If kids can grasp this point as they enter the application fray, if they can keep from being put off by the random aspects of the college mail business, these possibilities can be both inspirational and comforting.

VIDEOS

If college mailings aren't perfect, the same can also be said of the videos that have proliferated on cassette, laser disc, and CD-ROM. Ironically, the initial problem with videos may be that we hold such high expectations for them. Eight or ten years ago, for example, my college counseling office was involved in a pilot program in which we leased a laser videodisc player in order to screen videos from over one hundred colleges that were very popular with our students.

It was an exciting moment for the office when we unpacked the apparatus and set it up. Now, we thought, students would be able to save time and money discovering the crucial "feel" of colleges from the comfort of their own high school. Eagerly, a group of us tuned in.

Terrific, we thought, as the pictures rolled and the music swelled. Here were beautiful campus shots, close-ups of students walking by, their expressions enhanced by some very lively Vivaldi violin music in the background. Next, we heard from an especially diverse group of kids, who were talking about how much the faculty cared about its students and how professors regularly jotted their home phone numbers on the blackboard. Then we saw faculty members teaching and heard them talking after class about how much they cared for their students. As the violins played on, we saw students bending over microscopes, speaking out in seminars, and sculpting clay. The video took us to athletic practices and play rehearsals. We saw a little homecoming football, a snippet of *Macbeth* performed in the round, and a dance recital. Then as the violins slowed, our tour finished up at the library, as the narrator told us how graduates of the college had taken the lessons learned on campus out into the world to forge successful careers.

It was an appealing and informative picture, so we eagerly played another and then another. Halfway through that third video, however, a funny thing happened. We had a strange feeling that we had seen this one already. There was a campus with kids walking along pathways, and there was that Vivaldi sawing away in the background, and then, and you might not believe this, there were kids talking about professors writing their phone numbers on the blackboard . . . Different college, different kids, but the picture was very much the same. After watching a little longer and even checking out a couple of other videos, we discovered that colleges, by and large, look more similar than they look different. And it isn't that the makers of these videos lack originality, it's that the actors and the sets are the same. College students, at least the ones they film, are largely the same age and look a lot alike in the way they dress. (After all, they are targeted with vigor by giant fashionmongers like Nike and J. Crew.) In most colleges, students study the same disciplines in much the same ways and are taught by faculties trained at the same graduate schools. With so many commonalities, it is hardly surprising that colleges seem alike, so much so that occasionally students can't keep them straight in their minds, even after they've applied.

Another thing that can confuse us is that we have primarily learned to think of colleges in a linear fashion, based on their selectivity. In this state of mind we often find ourselves putting our brains through all sorts of contortions so we will see things the way we expect them to be. When, for instance, we tour Swarthmore and Haverford in quick succession, we expect to see that Swarthmore is better than Haverford in every detail because we know it is slightly more selective. With this linear mind-set operating, we trick ourselves into thinking that everything about a school ten places higher on the list will be demonstrably ten times better. We are surprised to find out that the variations are often minute, much smaller than the selectivity spread that is so clearly delineated in our minds. When we tour campuses, these mental contortions disconcert and exhaust us. It sounds ridiculous, but people in the grip of this mental state can expend considerable energy trying to believe that Swarthmore must have better sidewalks than Haverford or nicer gymnasium foyers (or whatever). Some people so badly want distinctions to exist that they even make them up.

For example, one day I was talking to a student about Dickinson College. I suggested he apply there because it is an excellent school where he had a good shot of gaining admission. After we had talked for a while, he revealed to me that he just couldn't apply to Dickinson, even though he agreed with me that it was a great school for him. He couldn't go to college there, he said, because he remembered from his visit that a major street went right through the Dickinson campus. This reasoning caught me by surprise, and for a minute I thought to myself, gee, maybe traffic safety is a problem. But then I looked down his list of colleges, and there were Williams and Amherst, campuses powerfully bisected by busy highways. I asked him if he remembered those roadways and he shook his head, leading me to conclude that if a school is regarded as prestigious enough, the very streets beneath our feet can be made to disappear.

This may seem like an overly skeptical critique of both videos and direct mail, and if I have slanted it that way, I do so in the hopes that readers will regard the marketing attempts of colleges as door-openers more than deal-closers.

CATALOGUES

There is, however, one resource that can be as helpful as it is underutilized: a college's own catalogue of course offerings and academic policies—the real user's manual. Years ago, colleges sent these out to all interested students as promotional material. But the lack of pictures, combined with high production costs, brought this practice to an end, and now catalogues are only sent to people who request them. Sometimes a small fee is charged, but it's worth every penny. Catalogues open the door to the academic life of a college. (If you are wary about clogging your mental and physical systems with still more college information, a good start might be to order only one catalogue from each type of college under consideration: e.g., a major research university, a small liberal arts college, a women's college, a service academy, a business college, an engineering school, and so on. Another approach is to find them on the Internet.

When you look at their contents, you will find that they can actually stimulate interesting conversations about the nature of college academics. To see what I mean by this, try comparing specific offerings in a given major across several different types of colleges. What might be the advantages of majoring in chemistry at an engineering school compared to the same major at a liberal arts college or, if appropriate, a women's college? How many art history professors does a small college have to employ to make it a viable major? Or how does a liberal arts college teach writing? You may be surprised by your discoveries—how few courses, for example, are required for some college majors or, perhaps, how few courses make up an entire undergraduate career.

Taking another tack, you might have questions about what courses undergraduate psychology majors take, what an anthropology major involves, or what mechanical engineers need to learn. The questions are endless. What does "double major" or "area studies" mean? Would a music major be better off at a college with a full-fledged symphony orchestra? What is out there in the way of year-abroad programs, what do they cost, and can students from College X earn credits from a program sponsored by College Y?

The possibilities for talk and learning will probably contribute to better decisions throughout a student's educational career. So don't be daunted by the small type or the academic jargon. The catalogue plunge is worth it, because this material shows us that an education can be more than a fancy diploma on the wall. It can (and should) be a toolbox of possibilities to help keep one's life in good running order.

What you will find in college catalogues is powerful information that can help you, the consumer, substantively differentiate between colleges. With a catalogue in hand, you will no longer attempt to conjure up differences between colleges by comparing ephemeral details like sidewalks or gymnasium foyers. Students, at the threshold of a very big and expensive decision, can use catalogues to draw useful distinctions and begin to picture, in their imaginations, their course through the maze of their own education. What they will gain by using this approach is  inestimable, and there is yet another by-product. Students who have read catalogues carefully enough to use the information these contain in interviews and essays are so rare that their questions and insights have the power to knock the socks off of admissions officers reviewing their cases.

COLLEGE SEARCH VIA COMPUTER

These days there are a lot of computer programs to guide students to specific colleges. Chances are your high school college office or library has one or more of them, or you can try the local library. Software is also available commercially from the College Board, Peterson's, or any of the major big-book publishers, and you can even access college search programs on the Internet. Once the data is collected, after all, it's not difficult to put it out there on disc or send it through cyberspace.

The advantage of computer searching is that kids love it; all the zap and bang that excites kids about computers (and makes their parents nervous) is built-in from the outset. Just type in the criteria you want—geographic parameters, academic programs, size, sports programs, financial aid, academic profiles—and zappo: there's your list . . . Well, maybe. Sometimes the data is faulty, and sometimes, if you put in something like lacrosse or geology or business administration, you might knock out a bunch of colleges you're interested in without ever knowing why.

Some people love computer-driven college searches and some people hate them. (Some of us, after all, think it's a miracle if we run into an old friend in a supermarket at random, while others of us wonder how many we might have missed by turning down the paper-towel aisle instead of heading for the canned fish.) Personally, I'm the type who worries about what I might be missing, so in addition to computer searches, I like to thumb around in big books to get the "feel" of what's out there in an area I'm researching, rather than let some computer protocol do it for me.

CYBERSPACE AND THE USES
OF THE COLLEGE WEB SITE

Although I am pretty lukewarm about the benefits of college search software, I have become increasingly enthusiastic about the college web sites that you can find on the World Wide Web. These web sites, when well-done (and many of them are), seem to be remarkably useful in helping us get a feel for a given college. In most instances, they contain a general introduction to the college, along with pictures of its campus, admissions information (often including an application that a prospective applicant can either download or complete right on the screen), as well as financial aid procedures.

And this is only the beginning. Good web sites have all sorts of other nuggets: week-to-week news about what's up on campus, sports stories, copies of the student newspaper, and often a complete copy of the course catalogue and academic schedule. Web sites can convey the "texture" of a given campus in a way that is not accessible with anything short of an actual visit. In part, this is because colleges often let their students speak for themselves, so the pages don't have the homogenized viewbook/video sameness that renders professionally contrived materials so bland and unengaging. Maybe all this will change—maybe the grownups will take over—but for the moment a lot of what colleges put on the screen has the power to bring you right to their campuses.

9

HOW TO TALK
ABOUT COLLEGE ADMISSIONS AT HOME

You may be puzzled by a separate section devoted to the subject of talking to your child, something you probably do a whole lot of, and I want to assure you that I am not trying to patronize here. I just know from personal experience, and from discussions with countless students and their parents, that college admissions can become a thorny and difficult subject to talk about at home. You start in on the subject as if it's going to be a regular sort of chat, and suddenly it's a volcano; either that or a black hole. Naturally, parents are surprised by the emotional intensity and short-circuiting that can become a standard feature when the "C" word is mentioned at home. As we have seen, at the heart of this eruption or collapse is anxiety over separation in conjunction with anxiety over the issue of winning and losing that college admissions represents.

As a family, therefore, we should enter this force field thoughtfully, our senses of humor at the ready. Also, from the outset we should acknowledge (because each child is different) that this will be a new journey for everyone. A business-meeting format complete with yellow pads and closely scripted agendas might work at the office, but it can be threatening at home. Kids feel vulnerable shuddering there on the threshold of what they view as the beginning of life itself; and because their genetic material seems to be so clearly on the line, parents can get pretty tense, too. So when the subject of admissions is brought up, it's wise to keep the talk general at first.

College settings can be a good starting point. In a discussion of rural versus urban, for example, right or wrong isn't so much the issue. It's just that some kids require twenty-four-hour access to pizza and get nervous walking on unpaved surfaces, while others need mountain-bike trails or rocks to scale. Talking through these differences enhances young people's sense of who they are and helps parents understand how their kids differ from themselves and each other. Furthermore, a fresh start helps each child feel like she or he is getting custom-tailored treatment rather than being dealt with as so much family sausage. Conversations starting with generalities about place can also set a collaborative tone that will prove particularly helpful in future discussions, when emotions may be running even higher— e.g., when deciding whether to take a better financial aid package at a less desirable college.

At the outset of discussions, a lot of the suburban kids I talk to say they want something in between urban and rural (something more like home), and we have fun talking through what they see themselves doing on weekends. What will they really want or need beyond their campus: a symphony subscription? Army-Navy surplus clothes? Thai food? Will cruising the mall be as much a part of their lives in college as it has been so far? In reality, will they have the time and money to shop till they drop?

Discussions like this enable kids to begin imagining their life on and off college campuses, maybe for the first time. Leisure time as a topic gives them a good place to start, because eleventh graders know more about hanging out than they do about college academics. Later on, everyone can talk about what majoring in experimental psychology might be like, but a subject like making use of a college's environs can get a conversation going.

Size can also be a "safe" and illuminating topic. Will the young person in question be more comfortable on a campus where kids say "hi" to nearly everyone on the pathways, or will he or she revel in the anonymity of a bigger campus, which allows a social life that isn't under the supervision of several hundred close friends and observers?

A discussion about size can also help kids figure out their particular learning styles. Your questions might be: Are you a student who's got to talk in every class? Is your hand up a lot? Do you want to express counter-opinions immediately? Or are you the sort who prefers to mull things over from the back row, content to let the experts lay out the parameters of a debate before forming your own ideas? Do you want regular feedback on projects, or are you happier with the challenge of putting together a piece of work on your own?

Everyone will have different responses to such questions,

and as answers develop, a sense of the "right" college size can begin to emerge—right there in the kitchen.

Not surprisingly, many parents find it hard to keep prejudices to themselves. Individually they may think of all rural areas as the boondocks or, conversely, be terrified that one of their children might end up walking on a city sidewalk at night. But it's best to keep these prejudices under wraps. If we do, it may encourage clear thinking about a very complex and emotionally laden subject.

Let's remember how sensitive kids are to our prejudices—even the prejudices they imagine we have. One common theme I hear from students during their junior year goes something like this: "I don't know why we're even talking about these other colleges 'cause Dad won't let me go anywhere but his place." It would be easy to think this comment reflects absolute reality. But then a month or so later, when I'm talking to the father, he'll say he's not pushing his alma mater at all. It's odd, but they can both be right.

The reason for the apparent contradiction is simple. Throughout their childhoods, the kids have heard ad nauseum about their father's glorious college days, when it never rained on football games and friendships were scripted by Hallmark cards. To add to this, when he attended reunions with his family, the kids heard a lot of good-humored remarks from his classmates about being chips off the old block, sure to follow in his footsteps. Of course, Dad took these remarks as so much cocktail party banter, but the kids heard this as their destiny writ in stone. As adolescents struggling to establish their own identities, it's not surprising they take exception to the idea that their father's harrumphing, purple-faced fraternity buddies have determined their life course. Although Dad may have care-

fully avoided making matriculation at his college seem pre-
ordained, the idea might have already imposed itself on his
children, especially if ever since they can remember he has
given them his alma mater's sweatshirts every fall.

Another risky parental role is that of family "contra-
rion"—the parent who sharpens the kids' wits by arguing
about every subject that comes up during mealtime. Applying this technique to the college subject can be particularly
tedious for kids. They can get confused enough on their
own. They don't need your help. Down the line there will
be plenty of time for all that, and with topics like drinking
and drugs, fraternities and sororities (or the lack of same),
coed bathrooms in the dorms, gay activism, date rape, and
over-the-edge political, journalistic, and artistic expression
as an essential part of the landscape of virtually every American college, there will be plenty of subject matter to keep
you all going. But now is not a good time. It's okay if soph-
istry is your style, but why not wait until after your kids have
matriculated, when their educations will make them wor-
thier opponents.

I don't mean parents should let their children rule every
decision; I am simply advocating a collaborative tone of dis-
course. Each family will have its potholes to steer around or
its bad roads to avoid completely, but if the approach is
right, it can't help but smooth out the ride.

With this in mind I once asked a skillful parent, whose
kids I had taught and grown to admire, how his family
seemed to work though major decisions so effectively. He
said that in talking with his kids he always tried to stick to
a basic question that went like this: "Where do you see yourself in five years (or ten, or twenty, or thirty), and what do
you think you are (or could be) doing to get there?" He

said the question had four advantages. First, it turned the problem under discussion over to where it rightly belonged, his children. Next, it invited a step-by-step approach. Third, the nature of the question encouraged responses that were conversational, not confrontational. Finally, this conversational quality made room for the opinions and observations of other family members, while still reserving ultimate responsibility for the protagonist.

At the end of my adolescence, I had to make decisions on my own about things that were zooming at me so fast it felt like bugs whacking into the windshield of a speeding car. I wish someone had helped me to slow down, so I could have seen further and more clearly into the darkness ahead. Certainly there's nothing like good talk at home for doing that, and you should remember that even though your kids might not invite conversation at every stage in the college admissions process, it can be useful and even fun when it happens.

10

ON THE ROAD

SOME OF THE THINGS THAT REALLY HAPPEN
ON COLLEGE VISITS

One way to break the logjam of college anxiety is to get out on the road—look under a few hoods, kick some tires. Keep it simple at first. Don't make a high-pressure trip to the presumed college of everyone's dreams right off. Practice a little looking first; learn what questions to ask. The modern college is a complex organism. On the first visit, you may be dazzled by new facilities, technology centers, comfy library chairs, health club amenities at the gym, and three-meal-a-day ice cream smorgasbords. Parents, particularly fathers of girls, might find themselves unnerved that different genders seem to share so many aspects of dormitory life. Kids may have trouble understanding the impact of big and small colleges until they have walked a few campuses and discovered that, on some really giant ones, a change of dorm might be necessary if you want to change majors—just so you can make it across campus in time for class. Decoding jargon and getting savvy about sales presentations are a big part of everyone's job here. Who knows, the first time you all take a campus tour, you may be so impressed that the tour guide is able to walk backward and talk about the distribution requirements at the same time that you notice little else.

Before you get started, here is an important thing to keep in mind: *Forget the admissions requirements of the college you are touring.* In other words, don't try to see everything through the lens of selectivity. If the B.U. tour guide on Wednesday seems smarter than the Penn tour guide you had on Tuesday, even though you know Penn is supposed to be harder to get into—let it go. Don't spend the entire visit trying to square your impressions with your preconceptions. Instead of obsessing about test scores, just try to see what you can see; it will help everyone relax and be at their best, and you will get a clearer view.

The cost of doing otherwise is high. Over the years I have talked with too many families who returned from extensive college visits with precious few insights to show for their time, effort, and expense, because all they seem to have done is recapitulate the selectivity pecking order in their minds. ("Princeton *is* better," they say. "You should see the lawns they have down there!") If you want to find that Penn is harder to get into than B.U. there are more efficient ways to go about it. The point of visits is to initiate a process of discovery in which kids can find out what is best for them.

If they walk through a campus dominated by feelings of either inferiority or superiority, they probably won't be learning much.

"But wait," you ask. "Isn't the admissions piece, the getting in, the most crucial part of the puzzle? Shouldn't we be using the trips to check on our chances, asking any admissions person we see what the deal is?"

Odd as it may seem, the answer is no. Too much doublespeak dominates this part of the business. These days the first job of every admissions office is to generate applications to their college. This in turn enables them to fulfill their second job: to reject as many of these applications as possible, which makes their college "selective" and, therefore, desirable in the marketplace. Keeping these dual tasks in mind, it's easy to see that being truthful with visiting applicants and their families is difficult. Although college people are neither untruthful nor sadistic, they need to generate high rejection numbers because their "percentage of accepted applicants" determines their college's rank in rating guides published by *U.S. News & World Report* and others. The lower the percentage of applicants a college accepts, the higher its ranking. And as we all know, these ratings make a huge difference to a college's status and subsequent success in the admissions marketplace.

For this reason college tourists should be skeptical when encouraged to apply. These days if a student asks an admission officer whether an application to the college will be worthwhile, the answer will almost always come back, "Yes." But what the officer probably means is that the application will be worthwhile to the college.

Of course, some admissions people have encouraged unrealistic applications for years. A decade or more ago, this phenomenon was most often explained by the youthfulness of rookie interviewers. Pumped up by their first summer on the job, these extroverts thought everyone they talked to looked good—all the more so because they had yet to spend a winter in the grind of reading and rejecting. The result was that each fall I'd be greeted in my office by a parade of seniors eager to tell me that the admissions officer they had just talked to at Williams, or Middlebury or wherever, had assured them he would love to have them apply. Naturally, they assumed, these words meant they were as good as in. But as a grizzled veteran of the bad news that April often brought with it, I remained skeptical, especially when these same students conceded, "Yeah, the admissions guy I talked to *did* look about my age."

Given the way the game is played now, rookies aren't the only ones inflating hopes. With the ever more pressing need to generate applications on their minds, even admissions office veterans are, as the following story demonstrates, required to spread a rosy glow to visitors.

Several years ago, the director of admissions at a well-known, very selective Eastern liberal arts college was summoned to the president's office. The president wanted to know if it was true the director had recently advised a high school visitor in an interview *not* to apply to the college. Yes, the director said, recalling the conversation in his mind, the student's record was so weak he thought further encouragement would be unethical. At this confession, the president, visibly peeved at the director's obvious lack of marketing savvy, told him that if he did this again, he would be through at the college. With the handwriting so clearly on the wall, the director resigned before the year was out.

BUT IF WE CAN'T COUNT ON WHAT ADMISSIONS PEOPLE SAY, WHY EVEN VISIT?

By now you're asking, why even visit a college? Why not just flip through the viewbook, catch the video, or check out the web site to see what the campus looks like? The answer is twofold. The simple fact of viewing facilities firsthand—pillars, lawns, dormitories, and so on—makes the college admissions undertaking seem real. Equally important, college touring, once underway, often serves to move students toward the exploration of more interior landscapes.

A road trip helps kids picture what leaving home and going off to college will actually be like. And more subtly, but just as important, it gives them a sense of what *they* might be like going off to a particular college. Somewhere in the midst of driving through new countryside, in filling the tank at distant gas stations or sitting back with a slice of pizza at a late-night campus joint, kids begin to understand the real journey they are undertaking. They glimpse themselves moving outward, taking charge, getting a grip on their educations, perhaps even on their lives. As they project themselves into the future, the lessons they learn are critical, not only to making good choices but to making those choices work when they finally end up at college. Although the dynamics of this process may seem obvious to parents, they are less so to young people. Given the jumble of hopes and fears simultaneously orbiting in the mind of a late adolescent, it takes sustained focus for kids to imagine the broad journey they are setting out on. A college tour begins to provide that focus.

• • •

When juniors first come to my office early on, before they have made actual college visits, their preconceptions are, of course, theoretical. If I ask what size colleges they are thinking about, the answer often comes back, "Big." Perhaps this means they really understand the advantages of a large university. But more likely it means that at winter's end of junior year, their high school (no matter its actual size) is seeming pretty small to them. They want more variety in classmates, prom dates, stuff to do. To many juniors, in early March "big" sounds good. But it may seem less so when these same students see bigness arrayed before them on a campus of 30,000 students, when they realize that in such a college their social security number, rather than their name, will often be the operable piece of information.

At this first meeting, we also talk about travel time from home. When I ask them about distance, they often say, "Far." But by the time they get to "far" on their visit, they know what the word means. They know it in actual tanks of gas (a particularly potent reality check in the mind of a teenager). Now, I'm not advocating either "small" or "near." What I'm saying is that after a road trip, attitudes change, perceptions sharpen; the question becomes a people thing, not just a data thing.

And for parents, there are changes as well. Often they tell me when they have returned from a college tour that, in the time capsule of car travel, their children grew before their eyes. Kids who didn't have a clue where they were headed suddenly got interested in road maps. Some even started pulling out the college catalogue before they arrived for an interview. And once they had seen a few campuses, once they heard their own voices actually speaking about their future to a stranger, they could begin to claim that future as their own. It's a vital time. Suddenly the Walkman earphones come off; conversations between parent and child go to new levels. These ice-breaking trips contain such magic that experienced parents, who have taken older siblings on tour, often vie with each other for the privilege of making trips as younger children get ready to hit the road.

WHO SHOULD GO?

So far, our discussion of college visits has assumed these will be family outings. But what about the question of kids traveling on their own? I've worked with amazing high school students who have gone about the college visiting process in complete independence. They do the research, set up their own appointments, and then come back with a unique understanding of what's out there for them. But mostly when kids talk about striking out on their own, what they mean is a bunch of them (usually guys) on the road. Not surprisingly, these road trips produce mixed results. One typical problem is that when such a group arrives on campus, the kids get so busy pretending they are students at the college (and not, heaven forbid, dorky high school tourists), that they don't learn much. For these kids, joining a formal tour or asking questions will surely blow their cover, so they mostly hang out in public places soaking up the aura in hopes that some really "hot chicks" will invite them to a party. Not only do these particular hopes rarely pan out, but clearly a campus visit of this sort doesn't uncover a lot of information about, say, the strength of the college's sociology department. Another problem with the "bunch of guys" approach is that there tends to be a lot of compromising about which colleges to visit. So afterward, when I talk with one of the group, I find out he spent most of the time visiting his friend's list: nice enough for an overview, but not so useful to his specific case.

In resolving the issue of peer versus family travel, parents should not cave in to kids who want to go on their own simply because they feel embarrassed at the prospect of being seen in public with grownups, especially their parents. Parents should feel comfortable in assuring their kids that families on tour have become such a fixture of the American college landscape that they are virtually invisible to undergraduates. Kids should understand their entire collegiate social life will not be doomed by a father's bad taste in sweaters or a mother's excruciating and humiliating follow-up questions about dormitory life. By the same token, parents should be aware that at this stage we are, ipso facto, an embarrassment to our children. (Remember that when Billy Joel's daughter was this age, she reportedly begged him not to play the piano in front of her friends.) So in exchange for allowing us to tag along, we parents should try as far as is humanly possible to tone down our middle-aged mannerisms, which have the power to turn the word "Dad" into that multi-syllabic sound "Deeeeaud!"

Finally, in thinking about who should go where and with whom, it's wise to rely on the family's way of doing things. If you've always talked through decisions together, then a joint trip is probably best. If independent action is the norm, going it alone might work better.

Down the line, things become clearer. In the winter of senior year, kids can learn a lot on solo visits, especially as they narrow their choices. At this point, staying over in a dorm with a friend (or with a student host arranged for by the admissions office) and visiting classes the next day can really help someone understand how a college ticks. Another good time for going alone is after acceptance letters have come in and decisions have to be nailed down. Recently, colleges have instituted accepted candidates programs—elaborate campus galas scheduled between March and April acceptance letters and the May 1st reply deadline. Although these programs naturally involve a good deal of yield-enhancing malarkey as colleges roll out the red rug to lure pre-freshmen, they can be particularly helpful to students on the horns of a multiple-acceptance dilemma. Faculty members representing different majors are available to talk to prospective candidates, and student organizations host events. These accepted candidates programs are even useful (and certainly fun) for those who have already decided which college to attend. With the admissions pressure lifted, kids are finally free to project themselves into the life of a college. Several months before leaving home, they can use a few days on campus to scope out potential friends, to get a feel for the ground beneath their feet, and to just plain get excited about the marvels that lie in store for them.

TIPS FOR KIDS ABOUT MAKING GOOD CAMPUS VISITS

1. Planning is key. As you shape up your list, pull out a road map. Be conservative about travel time between campuses. Don't set up a frantic pace that turns the trip into a blur. Where an interview and a tour are included, two to three hours per campus is the rule of thumb.
2. Be sure to call ahead to arrange interviews and to find

out the times of campus tours and group sessions. The receptionist you speak to will know *exactly* how long it will take you to get to neighboring colleges. Don't be embarrassed to ask the people at Bowdoin about getting to Bates; (or LL Bean for that matter); they give this sort of advice all day long. And because an applicant's interest in an institution is often deduced by whether or not he makes a formal visit to campus, you also want to be in touch with the admissions office. In an era of multiple applications, when it comes to a close call, colleges often accept the kids who have shown an interest in them. So if you visit, make sure you get counted.

3. Read up before you go. It will save you time and money in deciding where to go and will help you know what you are looking at when you arrive on campus. Reading also stimulates useful questions and makes you into the informed consumer you should be.

4. Talk to people involved with your special interests: coaches, professors, activities coordinators, orchestra conductors, studio artists. Professors in undersubscribed majors (e.g., Classics) are particularly interested in connecting with students who might beef up their departmental enrollments. These specialists can become advocates for you in the process. Get their names and E-mail addresses from the admissions office and make contact before you arrive.

5. Interviews are not contests between you and a person in a suit; they are a chance for dialogue. Few, if any, high school students talk their way into (or out of) a college, so you probably won't either. Just relax, and

make a friend whom you can call with questions or to straighten out snafus. (Of course, to make this work, you'll have to get the person's name. Writing in care of the "short bald guy" you talked to in the admissions office might not produce the effect you desire.)

6. Be comfortable on the campus. You are not the first young person to walk across it in the company of middle-aged people, and you will be surprised at how willing college kids are to talk to you and your family. Most, in fact, love to discuss their experiences. Also, it's okay to poke around the campus after the tour— pick up a copy of the newspaper, have lunch in the snack bar, visit the bookstore to get a feel for the kind of texts you might be reading in a specific course that interests you. Keep in mind that, even as you are looking at a specific college, you are also learning what a college education is all is about.

7. Finally, it's okay to be tired. Projecting yourself into four years of walking these paths, living in these dorm rooms, or eating in these dining halls is an exhausting process. Go back to the bed-and-breakfast for a nap. Spread out your visits to allow for simple fatigue.

USING YOUR COLLEGE COUNSELOR
EFFECTIVELY

THE CAPED-CRUSADER PROBLEM

As a college counselor in a high school, whenever I attend a school athletic contest or play and stand watching the action along the sidelines or chatting with folks between the acts, I often get the feeling that parents (either consciously or unconsciously) ascribe supernatural powers to me. To parents at independent schools or high schools with a low student-counselor ratio, we college counselors seem to have inordinate control over the future of their children. They know we write school recommendations to colleges, and they have noted the check boxes at the bottom of most applications in which we are asked to rate the academic and personal qualities of their children, from "below average" all the way to "one of the best I have seen in my career." Furthermore, they may have seen us greet admissions officers as old friends at college nights or college fairs, and they know some of us attend meetings in distant cities with admissions directors. As if these things weren't enough, they have heard that at crunch time we make mysterious phone calls—phone calls that, if they let their imaginations (and their paranoia) run free enough, surely decide everything. It is little wonder they begin thinking of us as omnipotent action figures who can influence a student's educational future mysteriously and uncontrollably. By the same token, when I feel the tingle of magic powers being ascribed to me from afar—beamed across some ball field or auditorium—it makes me edgy and uncomfortable. I think of it as the caped-crusader problem—this wish on the part of well-meaning parents to think that at the heart of the admissions muddle there is a wizard.

So what is the truth? Who are school counselors? What do we do? What powers do we wield? How do we affect a student's chances?

The answer to the "who are we" question is easy. Mostly, we do the jobs we do because we like kids. We find it interesting and challenging to help them work through what, for many of them, is their first major life decision. As we get to know a new crop of high school juniors every year, we enjoy the collaborative process of discovering which interests and strengths each individual brings to our office. Often, the kids we work with haven't recognized what they have going for themselves, and it's fun to help them discover it, to talk through its implications, and to get them started on appropriate visits and college essays. If we do our jobs as counselors right, by senior year the kids we work with don't think of us as anything close to caped crusaders. To them we are simply people who are there to help.

I have been lucky to have worked in schools where such relationships are possible, something that is much more difficult to accomplish in large public high schools, where the student-counselor ratio is often more than several hundred to one. When parents come to school to talk to us about college admissions possibilities for their children, they rarely know us like their kids do, which makes it easy for them to think of our office as the spot where deals get made, or to ascribe to us vaster powers than we have. Needless to say, such preconceptions clutter the picture. So let's take a look at a couple of parent-counselor meetings.

It's spring, and Emily, a junior at Southwood High School, has just met with her counselor. They have talked about her academic career, her extracurricular involvement at school, and what she has done over the summers. They have also talked about her basic learning style (she likes classes where she can really get involved in discussion) and her sense of the ideal college for her in terms of size and geographic setting (small, rural, northeast). She has also been able to discuss which of her nonacademic interests she hopes to continue in college. Finally, Emily and her counselor have constructed a tentative list of college options for her to explore based on her own ideas and the counselor's suggestions. Emily has told her parents, Doug and Vi, about her upcoming meeting with the counselor, so they eagerly await her report of how it went when they get home in the evening.

With little preliminary discussion, Doug and Vi demand to see the list of colleges, which, reluctantly, Emily produces from her front pocket. It's hardly an impressive document, this scrunched and tattered fragment of notebook paper penned in Emily's tiny script. But to Doug and Vi, it's the blueprint of Emily's future. Leaping on it, they don't take long to discover colleges whose names they either regard lightly or have never heard of at all. Tensions rise. Phrases like "If he thinks I'll pay for . . ." hang in the air. Emily recedes into the background, becoming little more than a bystander, as Doug and Vi pound away at their discontents.

Naturally, things are tense when Doug and Vi enter the counselor's office a week or so later. This couple feels insulted, testy. Doug sits ultra-straight in his chair and keeps snapping the creases on his trousers like a highly paid basketball coach who has just been assessed a technical foul. Vi is all over the place emotionally. She feels hurt. She's worried about Doug—he hasn't been sleeping well lately and he could really blow his top. And because she was never any great shakes in school herself, Vi feels guilty that Emily isn't an outstanding student. Clearly, neither Doug nor Vi understands what the counselor's job is. Without knowing him or hearing what he has to say, they have already appointed him as some sort of lord high designator, capable of getting any child into any college if he wants to. In this meeting they intend to show him that his list of colleges is *wrong* and to make it clear to him that his job is to get Emily into a college that is *right.* After all, they moved to Southwood especially so that Emily could attend this high school and get precisely this kind of service. And that move wasn't cheap.

Implicit in their approach is that Doug and Vi are people in search of the "special deal" they just know is out there for them if only they look hard enough. In this quest they remind me of my short career as a Christmas tree salesman during college vacations. It was long ago—back in the era when wild, unpruned trees were shipped south, pretty much *au naturel*, from the Canadian woods—and the specimens that we had to sell in the lot behind the lumber yard were scruffy stuff. This usually meant that hour after hour my sales associates and I would stand, holding up trees so grumpy customers could get a better look, as our feet froze to the ground and our fingers assumed a near permanent attitude of trunk clench. So after a while we developed a technique for satisfying even our finickiest patrons. What we did was to stock a little shed on the corner of the lot with a bunch of trees selected at random from our inventory. When a customer was really driving us crazy looking at tree after tree, we would finally allow that "Actually, sir, we *do* have some special stuff back there in the shed." Then with a gesture and a wink, we'd take them for a look-see. It was usually quite dark in there and nearly impossible to step back far enough for a full view, but the whole back-shed experience had such a special-deal aroma that those customers who wouldn't settle for anything less usually went away satisfied, no matter how spindly the tree.

Just like my Christmas tree customers, Doug and Vi are looking for the back shed of this college admissions business, and for them the counselor's office is the place. Given these assumptions, their visit will be tricky, especially if the counselor doesn't pick up on Doug and Vi's anger right off. But worse than the trickiness will be the time and motion wasted sparring over phantom issues and misplaced assumptions, while Emily, the young person with the future, goes virtually unnoticed.

So let's look at another family to see what we can learn. This time the student is Lydia, and to keep it simple, we will give her the same academic profile as Emily.

When they get home from work, Lydia's parents, George and Sherry, urge her to describe her meeting with the counselor from start to finish. They understand that an appointment with a man she doesn't know very well is a big deal to her, especially one that concerns something as important as her future education. Not only do they want to know how the meeting went, they make sure to understand the context of what was said. After a while, Lydia volunteers her list, and although they are startled by several college names with which they are only dimly familiar, they don't telegraph their dismay to Lydia at the time. Instead, they say it looks like they all have a lot to learn as the project moves ahead.

When George and Sherry enter the counselor's office, the atmosphere is quite different. For one thing, they have talked through their goals for the meeting beforehand. Primarily, they want to discover how well the counselor knows Lydia, not as a challenge to his professional expertise but to help him fill in gaps in his understanding and enable him to see Lydia in the context of her whole life, not just high school. Their second goal is to learn how the counselor intends to present Lydia (what some people call packaging) in the school letter he will write to colleges. As they discuss this, they intend to share with him the fact that Lydia has a severely handicapped younger brother named Jimmy, whom she has cared for with steadfast tenderness since she was a little girl. This information is relevant on several scores. It shows what sort of person Lydia is, and it explains her relative lack of after-school activities, because Lydia regularly chooses to go straight home from school to help with her brother until her parents get back from work. This information is new to the counselor, and he mentions his surprise that Lydia never told him about her brother. To this

George and Sherry are able to say that caring for Jimmy has become such a natural part of Lydia's life that she doesn't think of it as a big deal. When he hears this, the counselor knows it's a story that could be fruitfully shared with admissions people in his school letter and probably in Lydia's essay as well—not as a sympathy-grabbing device, but because her understated loyalty to her brother so clearly illuminates her character.

George and Sherry's third goal is to discover if the counselor has any particularly good college matchups in mind for Lydia, given her set of interests and abilities. Because it brings the counselor's expertise to bear on the specifics of the case, this is a valuable question that unites the parents and the counselor on the question of Lydia's future. He suggests a few colleges and says that when he and Lydia meet again he will, because of her experience with Jimmy, raise the possibility of schools that have programs preparing students to work with special-needs children.

George and Sherry show us the advantages of respecting process and of keeping focused on the whole picture. Who knows, Emily might have an experience as powerful as Lydia's care for her brother, but the counselor, given her parent's approach, isn't going to hear about it. You may be thinking I have stacked the deck in favor of Lydia, and in a sense I have. Obviously, our children may not have a story as compelling as Lydia's. Nevertheless, it is my experience that if both parents and counselors take time to discover each child's interests and hopes, as well as tapping into the experiences kids have treasured throughout their lifetimes, stories do emerge: stories young people can build a future around, if we give them the chance.

So when we ask a seventeen-year-old what he wants to be

and all he comes back with is "Happy," don't just leave it at that. And don't by any means accuse him of superficiality. Invariably his hopes run deeper, and if we are curious and patient, we can help him find the words to describe them.

UNDERSTANDING THE COUNSELOR'S DUAL ROLE

It's the fall of his senior year when Sean comes into my office to discuss how last summer's visits to colleges went and to shape up the list of schools where he definitely intends to apply. Ever since the spring of his junior year, when we first met, Sean has wanted to go to Williams—but he also liked Dartmouth, Amherst, and Princeton. His SATs are 680 verbal and 700 math. He has a 3.8 average in a strong group of courses, which includes AP Biology, AP American History, and five years of Spanish. He made the varsity soccer squad as a junior and hopes to earn a starting berth this fall. He is the sports editor of the school newspaper, and for the past two summers he has worked on the grounds crew of one of the local country clubs. Everyone likes this kid, so much so that several of his teachers volunteered to write recommendations for him at the end of their courses last spring. In many ways he is the heart and soul of his school: smart, energetic, a go-to guy who stays to clean up after dances.

But for all his energy and intelligence, Sean is not a shoo-in at Williams—or Dartmouth, Amherst, or Princeton for that matter. He's got a shot, definitely, but it's not a sure thing. So since our first meeting in the spring, I've been trying to get him to look into places like Middlebury, Hamilton, Colby, and Colgate; schools that share many of the qualities Sean likes about Williams, but which aren't so difficult to get into. But each time I mention these, I notice he looks hurt. When he tells me in the fall of his senior year that he hasn't followed up any of my suggestions with visits over the summer, I am worried. It's time to deal.

So I ask Sean, "Do you think I want you to apply to those other colleges because I can't recommend you to Williams?"

"Well, it kinda seems that way," he mutters, eyes down. "I mean every time I come in here, all you want to talk about is colleges I don't really want to go to. Maybe you've got Williams saved for somebody else."

"Boy," I answer, "I guess it could sound that way. But that's not it. Really. Not even close. My job isn't to decide who goes to Williams—even if it sometimes seems that way. I just want to make sure that if Williams doesn't work out for you next spring, you have choices. You're a great kid and a great student. You've earned the right to choices, and I want to make sure you have them if you need them."

At this, he brightens up. It's difficult to understand the dual role counselors play, but now he is beginning to see that I have two jobs. On the one hand, I am obliged to be a cold-blooded actuarial (complete with a green eyeshade, perhaps), who can provide a realistic assessment of his chances at various colleges. On the other, I am his advocate to the point that I can recommend him enthusiastically to a college he might not get into. When he understands that, instead of leaving my office thinking of me as his personal dream-buster, Sean knows we are working together.

SO WHAT DO WE DO, ANYWAY?

Although there are always some families who insist on keeping the caped-crusader label pinned to their college counselor all the way through the admissions cycle, the fact is that counselors can only help the kids they work with the "old-fashioned way"—getting to know them well and then effectively transmitting what we have learned. This transmission can happen in an official school letter to colleges, or when college admissions officers visit the high school; it can also happen in phone calls that make sure colleges have a clear picture of each applicant.

Such communication is often useful. But let's not go too far in our hopes for its power to launch kids into glittering colleges that otherwise would be beyond their reach. Let's not think it's like the old days, before the late 1960s, when headmasters at elite schools routinely told Ivy League colleges which of their students would, for example, "be coming down to New Haven in the fall."

It's certainly not like the days when Deerfield Academy's legendary headmaster Frank Boyden managed the college plans of his students, but this story from the 1950s is worth repeating anyway. It was back when Deerfield pioneered the recruitment of large and mobile public school postgraduates, whose size and skill guaranteed the Academy's longtime domination of its New England football league. As it happened one year, a member of a state championship football team received a full scholarship to take an additional year as a postgraduate at Deerfield. When a teammate's father heard about the deal, he thought an additional year of academic seasoning might also be a good idea for his son, even though the boy had already been accepted to Dartmouth.

So after a call to Boyden, both of the strapping lads went off to Deerfield, guaranteeing the Academy another great season. But Deerfield football wasn't the headmaster's only preoccupation. As a loyal alumnus of Amherst, he felt it was his duty to send one big lineman to his alma mater every year, and the young man already slated for Dartmouth seemed like the perfect choice. So after the season, the headmaster called the boy in and asked him if he would like to attend Amherst next year.

"Gee, Mr. Boyden," he said, "that sounds great, but I've already been accepted to Dartmouth, and I guess I'll be going there."

Remarkable as this might seem, to Boyden, this Dartmouth acceptance was little more than a detail that could easily be corrected with a couple of phone calls. And being one of the all-time great persuaders, it didn't take him long to convince the lad that reapplying to Dartmouth *and* applying to Amherst would be in his best interest. Later that spring when the letters came out, a strange thing happened: the boy was accepted to Amherst but not (because of Boyden's call) to Dartmouth, so Amherst is where he went.

Clearly, the world has changed. The most selective colleges have developed national applicant pools that render them largely immune to the machinations of prep school headmasters like Frank Boyden. Now, even the most powerful prep schools and affluent suburban high schools take what they can get in the way of acceptances from the nation's elite colleges. But this doesn't mean that college counselors in these schools don't keep working on behalf of their kids. Visits and phone calls are made to admissions offices in February every year, and colleges continue to be courteous to those high school counselors who represent some of the most talented students and athletes in the country. But these selective colleges don't roll over and give us anything we want.

Another reason counselors feel there is good cause to go through with visits and calls is that it keeps college admissions officers paying attention. If the officers know we are on top of things, that they will be asked to justify their decisions, they might be more careful about how these decisions are made. The imminence of a call or visit also motivates admissions officers to look over a given school's group as a whole, to make sure their decisions make sense back at the sending school. If, for example, an Ivy League college is dying to accept a high school's all-state quarterback, it might be talked into taking the class valedictorian as well. Or then again, it might not. But from a counselor's point of view, it never hurts to call and remind them of the valedictorian's case.

In my long experience of visiting and calling college admissions offices, as well as talking to colleagues at other schools about what they do, I can say the gains we make on behalf of our kids are incremental, and certainly students from schools that don't make these calls should not despair. (In recent years, in fact, several admissions offices—Princeton and Stanford, for instance—have stopped taking calls from school counselors, and other offices, such as Wesleyan University's, feel a special obligation to keep the playing field as level as possible for those applicants without telemarketing support.) Mostly, what we callers accomplish is to work the seams between an acceptance and a Wait List, and a Wait List and a denial. Because we know our kids well, we've got stories to tell admissions people about the small triumphs and tragedies they have weathered in the past year. Because we attend school events, we can be knowledgeable and effective advocates for the extracurricular talents of our students. When questions arise, we can explain an occasional drop in grades or underline a recent come-back. And always, we can help colleges frame their decisions within the context of our school's culture. Finally, we can listen closely to our colleagues on the other side of the ad-missions desk to hear what their needs are, so we can try for better matchups next year.

PART 4

MAKING THE SYSTEM WORK FOR YOU

12

SATS OR THE COLLEGE BOARD CONUNDRUM

Nowhere is the college admissions mystique made more manifest than in the workings of the College Board–Educational Testing Service. In its vast, intertwined administrative machinery (if ETS creates and administers the tests, what does the College Board do?) and its arcane and capricious terminology (is it a Scholastic Aptitude Test or a Scholastic Assessment Test?), juxtaposed with its schoolmarmish insistence on precision (make no stray marks!), this system has emerged in the national imagination as both an austere teacher who can never be fooled and a veritable Wizard of Oz to whom we go to for our pair of numbers (verbal and math). And these numbers, for good or for ill (in truth or in falsity), will whisper darkly to us about who we are for the rest of our lives. To add to the confusion, many people (and even some colleges) are saying that these days College Boards (or SATs or SAT IIs or ACTs or whatever you want to call them) don't even matter anymore.

With so much confusion over college admissions testing, what is the real story? Will testing be around for a while or will it just go away? And what, in the final analysis, should individuals do about it?

First of all, I don't believe that standardized testing as provided by the College Board or its competitor, the American College Testing Program—no matter how potent the arguments against it—will soon disappear as a major factor in college admissions. It is simply too big a business. With annual revenues in excess of $200,000,000, chief-executive salaries in the $350,000 range (plus housing allowance), and large, highly paid staffs (many of whom work in the opulent, campuslike ETS office park in Princeton, New Jersey), the College Board/ETS complex should prove to be about as durable an institution as the military-industrial complex.

As a college counselor at a Member School for years, I have attended regional and annual meetings and have watched in awe as dedicated and talented College Board bureaucrats alternately fawned over and flimflammed the membership that ostensibly controlled them. And then, when the meetings were over, the College Board employees returned to their offices and did exactly what they wanted to do—which was to build programs whose profitability and "indispensability" would further entrench individual and collective power. How else can one explain an institution that maintained for decades that it's tests were "coach-proof" and then, when this claim was finally discredited by independent researchers working with College Board data, rushed into the coaching business with its own brand of coaching software (called One-on-One: Test Prep from the Test Maker) to compete with commercial outfits like Arco, the Princeton Review, and Kaplan?

To illustrate the Board's independence from its membership, let me tell you about the time its Middle States regional office invited me and several other high school counselors to Philadelphia to discuss why we thought attendance was so low at seminars the Board sponsored for counselors around the region every fall. The reason for the poor turnout was easy to explain: the seminar agendas failed to address issues of any real interest to high school counselors. With this said, it seemed only natural to help them come up with interesting and useful programs. So for several days—all the while nibbling corporate Danish and dining out in the evenings, all expenses paid—we worked to create a list of compelling and important topics that would surely draw counselors to the following year's seminars. As we built the list, we thought we could feel a rising tide of discomfort on the part of the Middle States staffers, but they were ever cordial throughout the discussion, ever ready to send out for another cheese platter. It wasn't until the following year, when they mailed out flyers announcing the next round of meetings, that we realized they had totally ignored our suggestions. What they had wanted was not compelling ideas for the membership to discuss; what they had wanted was for us to help them come up with a forum in which they could market new programs to their membership. And when we took a look at the flyers and saw what they had put together by themselves after we left, we could see clearly that this was what they had wanted from the outset. When I think back on those three days in Philadelphia, I have a hard time believing that an institution so steadfastly concerned with marketing itself, no matter its nonprofit status, is likely to slide "gently" into obsolescence.

But for all its bureaucratic skill—even its willingness to fund buffets for naïve and idealistic high school counselors accustomed to cafeteria chow—the College Board (and to a lesser extent the American College Testing Program) has come under increasing attack. The locus of the criticism is a Cambridge, Massachusetts, group called Fairtest: the National Center for Fair and Open Testing. Its critique of the SAT goes as follows:

1. Fairtest says the SAT is "inaccurate," because among other things it "underrates the abilities of girls," who earn academic grades that are higher than boys' in both high school and college but whose SATs are lower—even with comparable preparation. If the job of the SATs is to predict college grades but its predictions are wrong for half of its test-takers, something, Fairtest argues, is amiss.

2. The SAT is "misused." By the College Board's own admission, each time a person takes an SAT, his or her total score varies by as much as 67 points, what psychometricians call the "standard error of measurement." This means that before one can establish a real difference between two individual test-takers, their scores must be as much as 140 points apart. Yet in spite of this "error of measurement," some colleges, the National College Athletic Association Clearing House (which determines if a student is eligible for Division I Athletics), and the National Merit Scholarship Corporation use "cutoff scores" such

that intervals as small as ten points make the difference between selection and deselection, between winning and losing, between playing and not playing.

3. Fairtest maintains that the SAT contains "biased context" and "biased language," by which students whose cultures render them unfamiliar with words like "regatta" or "shareholder" are penalized.

4. The SAT is based on a "biased format," Fairtest says, because its "timed, speeded nature works against young women and members of minority groups." "Guessing," it goes on, "is also a barrier for women [because] . . . the forced-choice format does not allow for shades of meaning, working against girls' more complex thinking style."

    In considering the implications of points 3 and 4, Bill Hiss, the dean of admissions at Bates College who spearheaded that college's decision to stop requiring the SAT, believes that the "test penalizes in rank order by the level of oppression." What he means here is that, arguably, African Americans have been oppressed the most and their scores are the lowest. Next in order come Hispanics, the children of blue-collar workers, rural youth, and, finally, women; all oppressed and all, in some fashion, discriminated against by the tests. (Clearly, this is an extremely complex and controversial subject well beyond the scope of this book, but nonetheless, it is worth thinking about as we try to assess the effects of the SAT not only on individuals but on the nation at large.)

5. The SAT is "coachable." What Fairtest will tell you is that, on average, good coaching raises scores by 100 points or more. Not only is coaching potentially costly

and therefore inherently unfair, but the fact that it works at all directly contradicts the mission of the test, which is to level the playing field for all test-takers. The College Board has always worked hard to downplay the effectiveness of coaching and in fact has denied for most of its existence that coaching works at all. For example, the director of the Board wrote in 1955 that "If the Board's tests can regularly be beaten through coaching then the Board is itself discredited." And in 1971, in a report with the hefty title "The College Board Admissions Testing Program: A Technical Report on Research and Development Activities Relating to the Scholastic Aptitude and the Achievement Tests," researchers concluded that "One of the principle aims in constructing the SAT is to make it resistant to attempts to increase scores by means of short-term cram courses. Indeed the usefulness of the SAT as an indicator of a student's potential for college work depends in large measure on the fact that the SAT measures general ability as it has developed over the full range of experiences in a person's life." But now, as noted above, the Board is firmly entrenched in the business of publishing coaching books and software, and even promotes its wares with such phrases as: "The only program with real questions," or, the one that really stands out, "With test tips from the test makers themselves."

In 1983, David Owen demonstrated in an article in *Harper's* magazine, and then in his devastating critique of the College Board entitled *None of the Above*, published by Houghton Mifflin two years later, that by becoming savvy about the "culture" of the SAT, a test-taker can reasonably expect to answer questions in a reading comprehension section correctly *by using only the list of answers provided.* *(See page 125.) What Owen shows us is that through coaching one can "learn" to take these tests. Now the College Board itself is telling us we can even learn from the people who make the tests—a case of the fox tutoring the chickens if there ever was one.

6. Finally, Fairtest says that SATs (or ACTs) don't contribute to better admissions decisions, because (as if this should surprise us) the high school record—what grades you get in what kinds of courses—works so effectively as a predictor of college performance that tests aren't even necessary in the selection of excellent students. To support this assertion, Fairtest often cites the well-known decisions by Bowdoin (1970) and Bates (1982) to abandon standardized tests as a requirement in admissions. Each of these colleges finds its "nonsubmitters" function in their classrooms just as well as its "submitters," and follow-up research at Bates reveals that nonsubmitters, *even though their SATs are 160 points lower than submitters,* earn grades that are only five one-hundredths of a point lower—2.84 versus 2.89. So much for the necessity of SATs as a predictor of college performance.

This leaves us with a final, pro-testing argument to discuss: the assertion that the SAT provides opportunity. Without a set of high scores on a nationally administered exam to help make a case to selective colleges in distant cities, this line of reasoning goes, won't that mythically brilliant kid from an unheard of high school somewhere west of the North Platte River remain undiscovered?

This is a legitimate worry. As a nation we need to develop all the talent we can, no matter how hidden it might be in the nooks and crannies of our sprawling educational system. But the trouble is that the SAT fails to do an adequate job when it comes to precisely these discoveries, because it fails to represent fairly the talents of the poor, the rural, and, as we have seen, the uncoached. In an ideal world, a test would exist to ferret out each diamond in the rough, but the present-day SAT, with all the shortcomings noted above, may not be the test.

WHY STANDARDIZED TESTS MIGHT BE AROUND FOR A WHILE

Yet for all the arguments one can marshal against SAT-type testing in college admissions, and despite the fact that colleges like Lafayette, Middlebury, Union, and Connecticut have recently joined the movement no longer to require SATs per se, there are a couple of reasons—more compelling than all the rest—why testing won't soon disappear. One reason is that the SAT plays a cardinal role in setting the pecking order among "top" colleges. Every year test averages published in various rating guides keep the "have" schools at the top of the selectivity heap simply because they guarantee that, the next year, kids with the highest scores will apply and then matriculate at these same colleges, thus locking in the status quo.

In effect the test becomes a marketing mechanism for "winning" colleges that pushes applicants toward the schools at the top of the score pyramid. Why on earth would these colleges have it any other way? Even if test scores consign a college to a specific level on the pyramid, why would it abandon such a golden recruiting mechanism, one that annually fills its coffers with freshly minted applicants, and then on May 1st makes accepted applicants leap, with hardly a question or a second look, at the college with the highest test-score average? Regardless of the questions individual administrators of these winning colleges might have about the efficacy or fairness of the tests, wouldn't asking them to drop SATs entirely be like asking Notre Dame to drop football?

Which leads us to a second reason why tests might be around for a while: our national obsession with lists of "bests." Perhaps because we lack a hereditary aristocracy to settle permanently the question of who's on top, we annually beat ourselves over the head with lists telling us who is the nation's best in virtually every field of endeavor—from pizza delivery to bad-hair days. We need not belabor this passion of ours to understand it. We need only ask what on earth we (or David Letterman) would do without ranking lists. Can we really imagine a nation without lists of "best colleges"—especially if we can be made to believe their validity is grounded in the "scientific" accuracy of standardized tests? Therefore, even though a few colleges are getting out of the testing business, I wouldn't advise waiting up late for places like Yale, Williams, Northwestern, Duke, and Stanford to jump on the test-free bandwagon.

THE TEST PREPARATION PUZZLE

"This is all very well," you are surely saying, "but all I want to know is whether I should be tutored or not."

Luckily—after a complex preamble—the answer about test prep is simple: get some, but don't go crazy.

These days even the more conservative observers in the field figure you can push up your total SAT score by something like 100 points if you work effectively at any type of test-preparation regimen. And you don't have to spend $500 or $700 or $1,200 on it either, because thanks to the New York State Truth in Testing Law, passed in 1979, you can buy test reprints of actual SATs or ACTs at your local bookstore. These tests come with answers and scoring keys, and are invaluable in helping you understand not only how the tests work but also what your strengths and weaknesses are. So take a few practice tests under timed, quiet conditions on some flat surface like your kitchen table; score them yourself and see where you stand. Next, get access to a computer and some test-prep software (available for under $40), and go for it.

Test prep helps you become familiar with multiple-choice formats, so that during the actual tests you won't have to struggle with decoding the *kinds* of questions the SAT or the ACT asks. It also helps with pacing, so that after a few practice sessions you won't be as likely to bog down in the middle of one section or finish too early on the next. Because of the way the College Board equates one test to the other, the sequence of questions on its tests always ascends from easy to difficult. Simply knowing this fact can help you figure out what sorts of questions you should bear down on and what sorts you might let go. Test prep can also help you develop a strategy for guesswork by teaching you the crucial skill of eliminating wrong answers before you take a shot.

If what I say about test prep makes it sound like testing is a just a game, you're catching on: that's exactly what it is.

That's why your best strategy is to learn how to play the game well. You may discover that you have to motivate yourself by signing up for an expensive course—just like a lot of us had to go out and buy pricey exercise equipment to keep us at it—but try not to go over the top. You don't have to spend your last dollar on elaborate courses or waste inordinate amounts of time in special classes. This testing deal is a game—some hoops to jump through on the way to where you really want to go.

And above everything else, remember that these tests don't have the power to tell you who you are. All they can do is tell you whether or not you are good at taking tests, which is a skill that you don't need very often. So approach the tests in good cheer, not all atremble, and keep in mind that the little man behind the curtain in the big testing palace is so confused that he doesn't know whether to call them Scholastic Aptitude Tests or Scholastic Assessment Tests.

*Anyone who has spent any time studying ETS tests (except, of course, anyone at ETS) knows that what is tested is primarily the ability to take ETS tests. In order to prove this to the readers of *Harper's* in 1983, I composed a short Scholastic Aptitude Test Aptitude Test (SATAT). The test, which I reproduce here, contains five items taken from a reading comprehension portion of an actual SAT. In answering them, reach back in your mind to the days when you took your own SATs and then look for the kinds of answers you think would appeal to a test writer at ETS.

Oh, yes; I've left out the reading passage that the items refer to. I've also changed the order of the items and eliminated all references to the actual novelist the reading passage discusses. And I've left out titles of any of the novelist's books. You need to know only that the novelist, though dead, has a name you would recognize, and that "the author" referred to in several of the items is the author of the reading passage, not the author of the novels.

So that you will approach this test in a properly anxious frame of mind, I will tell you that when I administered it to myself, after many hours spent reading SATs, I had no trouble getting all of them right. And I *still* haven't read the passage. When I administered the SATAT to four people at a *Harper's* editorial meeting, the youngest member of the staff, who had just emerged from the world of ETS exams, also got all the answers. The editor got three correct, a very respectable score, as did the political editor. The worst score—one out of five—was that of an editor from England who had never taken, or even seen, an SAT. (You'll find the answers at the end of the test.)

---

1. The main idea of the passage is that

   (A) a constricted view of [this novel] is natural and acceptable
   (B) a novel should not depict a vanished society
   (C) a good novel is an intellectual rather than an emotional experience
   (D) many readers have seen only the comedy [in this novel]
   (E) [this novel] should be read with sensitivity and an open mind

2. The author's attitude toward someone who "enjoys [this novel] and then remarks 'but of course it has no relevance today' " (lines 21–22) can best be described as one of

   (A) amusement
   (B) astonishment
   (C) disapproval
   (D) resignation
   (E) ambivalence

3. The author [of the passage] implies that a work of art is properly judged on the basis of its

   (A) universality of human experience truthfully recorded
   (B) popularity and critical acclaim in its own age
   (C) openness to varied interpretations, including seeming contradictory ones
   (D) avoidance of political and social issues of minor importance

(E) continued popularity through different eras and with different societies

4. It can be inferred that the author [of the passage] considers the question stated and restated in lines 8–13 to be unsatisfactory because it

(A) fails to assume that society and its standards are the proper concern of a novel
(B) neglects to assume that the novel is a definable art form
(C) suggests that our society and [this novelist's] are quite different
(D) fails to emphasize [this novelist's] influence on modern writers
(E) wrongly states the criteria for judging a novel's worth

5. The author [of the passage] would probably disagree with those critics or readers who find that the society in [this novelist's] novels is

(A) unsympathetic
(B) uninteresting
(C) crude
(D) authoritarian
(E) provincial

Answers: 1. (E), 2. (C), 3. (A), 4. (E), 5. (B).

—David Owen, *None of the Above*

13

BEYOND SAT: MULTIPLE INTELLIGENCES

Over the course of growing up, a lot of us have discovered it isn't just the "smart kids" who do quite nicely in life. Sure, it never hurts to be a "brain," but when we scan the local newspaper or go to a high school reunion, we often discover that some of the most potent success stories we hear are about classmates whose SATs were on the medium side, or lower. To those of us who have spent years working in schools or colleges, the irony of this is even more pronounced—especially to those involved in raising money from alumni. Decade after decade we keep finding that great success often comes to students with abilities that cannot accurately be measured by tests. (In fact, I'd be living in Aspen right now, instead of pecking away at this book, if I'd collected twenty bucks from every guy in a thousand-dollar suit who, when talking about his child's college prospects, sheepishly admitted that his own SAT scores weren't great either.) And it isn't just financial success we're talking about; it is the talents of successful artists, musicians, dancers, doctors, scientists, architects, and craftsmen that often go unrecognized in the testing process. Real life is full of stories about engineers who have a special knack for solving problems because of their unique way of seeing things, or therapists who bring what appears to be an almost God-given insight and empathy to their work, or surgeons who possess a special touch. And if we dig a little deeper, we find out that, because of low testing patterns, these people had to strike outside traditional definitions of talent to find their special niche.

In spite of what we know about the multidimensional aspects of success in the world, as a society we have stuck close to orthodox, standardized measurements as a basic yardstick. At the dawn of the twentieth century, a Frenchman named Alfred Binet came up with a test to assess the intellectual ability of Parisian schoolchildren—a test that evolved into the IQ test. Ever since then, we have placed increasing faith in the power of pencil-and-paper tests, administered on a mass scale, to deduce the intellectual raw material, the "intelligence" of a human being.

Most often these tests (and there are hundreds of them) focus on linguistic and logical-mathematical intelligence, not so much because these are the only areas worth finding out about, but because these areas are eminently testable. This testability makes the scores seem legitimate and clean, too—a single IQ number or an SAT total. The tests are cheap, have a scientific aura, and appeal to the nation's need to believe that "the best and the brightest" among us really do run the show.

The trouble is that the people running the show don't seem to be that smart—at least as measured by these verbal and math tests. So what kind of smart are they? Until 1983, there wasn't a systematic answer to this question. Then along came Howard Gardner, a researcher at the Harvard School of Education, who hypothesized that measuring linguistic and logical-mathematical intelligences was fine as far as it went, but that there were other areas of intelligence that were just as important. In his book *Frames of Mind: The Theory of Multiple Intelligences*, he outlined five other areas.

According to Gardner, *spatial intelligence* is the ability to see dimensionally in space, to be able to turn a drawing on its head and see it in three dimensions, to understand the globe or a downtown neighborhood as a map. *Musical intelligence* is just that (what Mozart had a lot of). *Bodily-kinesthetic intelligence* is the special intelligence that athletes, dancers, and brain surgeons have. It is the ability to engage one's whole body in the solution of a problem—like when Michael Jordan leaves the ground at the foul line and somehow arrives at the basket with the ball a little while later. *Interpersonal intelligence* is the skill of knowing how others feel, of helping people work together. *Intrapersonal intelligence* is the ability to know oneself.

Almost by instinct, we know that Gardner has made a very helpful breakthrough in the way we understand each other and ourselves. To use his phrase, this is a "pluralistic view of the mind," which recognizes that each of us has different ways of learning, contrasting styles of coping, a wholly original circuitry of responses to given situations or challenges. If schoolchildren could feel that they have many intelligences available to them—instead of the much-tested two—imagine the effect this insight would have on their self-esteem, imagine the possibilities for the way we educate and the way colleges make decisions.

Twenty-five years ago—a decade before Gardner's work—when I was starting my career as a college counselor, I had a long discussion with the director of admissions at the Rhode Island School of Design about why he had denied admission to one of my students, a marvelous artist who had submitted what many regarded as a stunning port-folio. "Yes," he allowed, "your student does seem to be a good artist, but his SATs don't qualify him for admission." When I asked what SATs had to do with success in art school, the director replied that RISD wanted only the "best" and felt the SATs could lead them to those students. Imagine the impact of Gardner's work on that type of thinking.

Subsequently, Gardner's ideas have been further elaborated by others, notably Daniel Goleman in his bestselling book *Emotional Intelligence*. Goleman makes a case for the kind of intelligence that is seated in our emotions, which has the power to determine how successful we are. In his words there are five keys to how emotional intelligence affects people's lives:

1. *Knowing one's emotions*. Self-awareness, recognizing a feeling *as it happens* . . . People with greater certainty about their feelings are better pilots of their lives,

having a surer sense of how they really feel about personal decisions from whom to marry to what job to take.

2. *Managing emotions.* Handling feelings so they are appropriate is an ability that builds self-awareness . . . People who are poor in this ability are constantly battling feelings of distress, while those who excel in it can bounce back more quickly from life's setbacks and upsets.

3. *Motivating oneself* . . . marshaling emotions in the service of a goal is essential for paying attention, for self-motivation and mastery, and for creativity. Emotional self-control—delaying gratification and stifling impulsiveness—underlies accomplishment of every sort . . .

4. *Recognizing emotions in others.* Empathy . . . is the fundamental people skill . . . People who are empathetic are more attuned to the subtle social signals that indicate what others need or want.

5. *Handling relationships.* The art of relationships is, in large part, skill in managing emotions in others . . . These are the abilities that undergird popularity, leadership and interpersonal effectiveness.

So before you put all your eggs in the test-preparation basket, think about the power that "emotional intelligence" can have to make life go well. And the best news is that these intelligences are not simply a matter of genetic destiny: they can be learned. Goleman shows us how stars in the workplace are people who have mastered building networks between key coworkers; how girls, by recognizing the difference between boredom and anger, can help themselves avoid eating disorders; how the schoolyard bully can be taught to read social clues more accurately and thus avoid feeling so threatened by his peers; how kids can be "coached" in the skills of friendship; and, finally, how a "winning sociability that draws people to them, self-confidence, an optimistic persistence in the face of failure and frustration, the ability to recover quickly from upsets, and an easygoing nature"—the very essence of emotional intelligence—helps people overcome even the most devastating emotional and social deficits.

Armed with the theory of "multiple intelligences" that I have briefly sketched above, maybe we won't be so surprised by who has succeeded and who has not when we return to a high school reunion in a couple of decades. And by the same token, when we judge youngsters, or ourselves, by the single and limited measure of the SATs, at least we should know that these tests are giving us only a small part of the total picture.

14

MONEY ON YOUR MIND

Few people can think about a college education for very long these days before the question of money pops up. Even a quick look at the price tag of a leading private college or university reveals that, short of a pretty severe drug habit or protracted medical care, there are not a lot of things a young person can get involved with that are more expensive. In spite of the hefty cost, however, many of us have put down large sums to educate our kids, because, in the long term, we feel there is little we can do for them that will so enrich their lives—literally and figuratively. Even with today's high prices, the dollars-and-cents case remains clearly in favor of a college education: in 1993, the Bureau of the Census reported that high school graduates had an average annual income of $19,422, while those with four-year college degrees earned $35,121. The case for wider vistas and a more interesting life, although harder to quantify, is probably even clearer. So in one way or another—for richer and certainly for poorer—people have paid for higher education in the past and will continue to pay in the future. This said, it doesn't mean we have to go like sheep into the scary wilderness of college costs. So let's see how smart we can become on the subject.

Right now it seems that you can best inform yourself about paying for college by using the Internet. (If this prospect seems daunting to you, chances are your child is more technologically adept than you, so this could be a good time to work together.) If you give it a shot, you should find the Internet is a fast, penetrating, and up-to-date tool. For a kaleidoscopic topic like financial aid—subject as it is to changes in political climate, bureaucratic whim, and the variable cost of money—the Internet's immediacy and relevance is incredibly useful. At this writing, the best single source of information about college money on the Web is called the Financial Aid Information Page, sponsored by the National Association of Student Financial Aid Administrators and run by Mark Kantrowitz (www.Finaid.org).

Features you will find on the Financial Aid Information Page include "more than a dozen financial aid calculators, including a college cost projector, a savings plan designer, a student loan advisor, and a loan payment calculator. They are all free, accurate, and completely confidential. Playing 'what-if' games with these calculators can provide you with a better understanding of higher education financing and help you plan for the future." It's reasonable to assume that the number and effectiveness of these sorts of tools can only grow in the future. (Recommending the Internet as a primary research tool, however, doesn't mean that you must buy a fancy computer and commit to a lot of expensive on-line services; the high school, the library, friends, relatives, or the workplace might provide you with all the access you need.)

TIPS ON HOW TO LEARN ABOUT FINANCIAL AID

1. Start early. If kids are reluctant to begin on the application part of college admissions, their parents are often equally slow about getting started on the money part; it's where the parents are being tested, and like their children, they can feel exposed. But remember, procrastination only makes things worse.

2. Learn to talk the financial aid talk. As with all bureaucratic undertakings, there's a new language to learn. At first it seems impenetrable, but it's just acronyms and jargon after all. Once you take the plunge, you'll soon get the hang of it.

3. Read everything you can on the subject. These days college costs are an annual whipping post for the national press. *Money Magazine, U.S. News & World Report,* and *Newsweek,* whose parent company also owns the Stanley Kaplan test-prep empire, are all deep into college news. These publications can give you the flavor of the current financial aid situation and provide useful tips about how and where to best use your money.

4. Be wary, curious, and use the tools available. As in any complex undertaking involving money, there are quickie schemes designed to get a little of yours. One of these is the scholarship search scam, whereby

you pay $25 to $50 to hear about sources of money—
millions of dollars which would go unused if you
didn't call a particular 800 number. Today! Every
year experts in the field claim you don't have to call
this number. They say you can find out about these
money sources free of charge from state and federal
government publications or other sources. For example, there is a free Internet service called
FastWEB that can link you to a searchable database
of more than 180,000 private-sector scholarships, fel-
lowships, grants, and loans. Another source is the
CollegeNET Mach25, which has a free Web version
of the Wintergreen/Orchard House scholarship
finder database that contains more than 500,000 private-sector awards from 1,570 sponsors.

5. Take advantage of free financial aid programs. Another resource to take advantage of are the "financial aid nights" and workshops sponsored by local
high schools, libraries, and colleges. Financial aid
professionals turn out regularly as a service, and
their presentations are interesting and helpful. They
come with a lot of useful handouts and are invariably
patient with the questions of newcomers to the process. Particularly useful are the handouts describing
qualification criteria, interest rates, and repayment
schedules of various loan programs.

6. Assess the real cost. It is increasingly common for
people to refer to financial aid as a system of dis-
counts, in which some students pay list price while
others pay less. As you begin applying to colleges, try
to look for the real cost that most students pay, not
just the sticker price. Magazines like the *U.S. News*

& World Report's financial aid issue attempt to provide this by listing a college's "average cost after
need award." (Discovering real prices might not tell
you the amount of aid you will receive, but it could
help reduce your chances of cardiac arrest as you
scan the prices.) The *U.S. News & World Report* issue
also lists colleges that generate the "most debt" and
the "least debt" among their graduates, and this
might help you get a sense of what you will be in for
at a particular school.

7. Devise a financial aid application strategy. Earlier, we
discussed application strategy solely in terms of admissions. Students who need serious money to attend college should also fashion a financial aid
strategy tailored to provide a variety of aid offers to
compare in April of their senior year. Since 1989,
when the Justice Department ruled that colleges
could no longer collaborate on the "packaging" of
individual financial aid awards, the money a student
receives will necessarily vary from college to college.
With no common set of criteria, each school arrives
at its own "expected parent contribution" and then
packages its award differently. In one, for example,
you might be awarded more outright grant money,
in another you might get mostly loans. There are
several reasons for these differences: the "method-
ology" used by aid officers is flexible, the aid budget
at each college is different, and, perhaps most important, some colleges are using financial aid dollars
as tools in the battle to fill their freshman classes
with the students they most want. In an April 1996
article on the subject, *The Wall Street Journal* reported

that "to achieve their ends these schools still start by calculating a student's demonstrated 'need'—determined by family income, assets and debt. Instead of stopping there, though, some schools then factor in dozens of variables that affect a student's propensity to attend the college once he or she is accepted. The higher the propensity, the less financial aid the student may expect. Factors can include the student's home state, ethnic background and area of study, and who initiated the first contact with the school." While it is probably impossible for you to try to anticipate to your own advantage the mathematical models that drive these strategies, it does make sense to anticipate varying amounts of aid by applying to a variety of colleges.

8. Consider the risks of asking for money. People assume that if you apply for aid, it materially reduces chances for admission. Happily, this is not the case. This said, however, college officials have admitted that Early Decision candidates sometimes are offered less money because their "propensity to attend" is so high. Another area where need plays a role is Wait Lists. By the time colleges take students off their Wait Lists, financial aid budgets are often spent, so admissions officials are forced to consider only full payers.

9. Remember: this is not the IRS. Even though the paperwork formats and terminology may remind you of income taxes and, indeed, you will be asked to corroborate your income and asset figures with tax returns, financial aid officers are not like IRS agents. In fact, many of them are among the kindest,

hardest-working professionals you will ever hope to meet. Sure they don't like to be conned, and they get tired of having so many conversations end up as negotiations, but these are people you can talk to, people who are interested in your explanations. So keep them informed, send them updates and revisions if your financial circumstances change, and trust them to do their best to make things work out for you at their college.

10. Don't just look at the total package, study its parts. When it comes to the choice of a college, you owe it to yourself and your children to examine each award carefully so that you understand the implications the debt may have. How, for example, will it impact the opportunities of younger siblings, the security of older parents, or the options of recent graduates? Just as with credit cards, it is now possible to borrow potentially destabilizing amounts of money, so be careful to assess the impact of long-term debt.

15

WHO GETS IN AND WHY

At first glance, college admissions seems like a relentlessly statistical enterprise dominated by test scores, application numbers, and yield percentages—a science. On second look, it appears to be so heavily laden with hocus-pocus that when people start talking about the subject, instead of staying within the bounds of specific data, they are soon fixated on mythical cases: a piccolo-playing cowgirl from Montana with a 520 verbal score gets admitted to Yale, while a New Jersey valedictorian with a 760 doesn't.

In the world of college admissions, the special quality that pulls an applicant into a class at a selective college, the thing that provides a distinguishing feature or edge, is called a "hook." In a sea of equally qualified eighteen-year-olds, such a differentiating factor can be crucial. Members of "underrepresented" minorities—(Hispanics, African Americans, and Native Americans) have hooks. Football players, alumni children, the sons and daughters of blue-collar workers, and "development cases" of interest to fund-raisers have hooks. Even some saintly child who helped her seventy-two-year-old grandmother hike the Appalachian Trail from Maine to Georgia might have a hook (at least if there isn't another applicant in the pool who helped her great-grandmother). When we hear about these hooks and the admissions miracles they produce, the stories don't seem to be about our kids—the ones who are always giving life their best shot, who have good grades and still make time to get the yearbook edited; the kind of kids who dig down deep and take AP Calculus, even though higher math is about as interesting to them as brussels sprouts. When people—ignorant of the laserlike omnipotence of hooks—talk about admissions, they usually end up with angry questions: Who's looking out for the regular, all-around kids? Kids like our kids? Aren't these all-American Toms and Marys, kids with no special claim to ethnic, economic, or geographic status, being unfairly sidetracked by a system in love with its own cute categories? And how on earth can we possibly make sense of the razzle-dazzle of contradictory decisions we hear about? How can we know who will be able to crack an admissions code that seems so random?

Naturally, college admissions officers have their answer to this set of questions, and their response boils down to this: "What we are looking for is not so much well-rounded people as a well-rounded class." For them, this is a great answer. It also covers a lot of bases.

First of all, it takes into account the idealism colleges have shown since the late 1960s in addressing questions of racial, ethnic, and economic imbalance. Few institutions in the political economy of our national culture have done as well as colleges in pursuing the goal of diversity—not labor unions or financial institutions or churches or neighborhoods. By some miracle of enlightened thinking at a couple of key institutions (Harvard and Amherst are notable in this regard), a majority of this nation's colleges have stopped being gatekeepers with a mission to bar the door against ethnic newcomers and other "undesirables." Instead, they have begun to encourage differences on their campuses by recognizing the educational disadvantages these groups faced and extending the benefit of the doubt as admissions decisions are made.

But the search for a "well-rounded class" goes beyond idealism on a college's part; it is pragmatic as well. Take the recruitment of working-class kids, surely a noble goal as the gap between white- and blue-collar America widens. Can it be regarded as an act of pure collegiate altruism if, year after year, so many blue-collar recruits turn out to be linebackers? And when does the admission of a cow-punching piccolo player become little more than a colorful story for admissions people to relate over dinner?

When it comes to special admits, particularly athletes, these numbers are not trivial. Until freshman football was abolished at Ivy League colleges in 1990, each college was allowed, under specifically drawn Ivy rules, to give admissions preference to fifty football players a year. When freshmen became eligible for varsity play, this number was reduced to thirty-five, and that is where the number stands today. According to highly placed sources in Ivy admissions offices, other sports get fewer "draft picks"—eight or ten for such sports as hockey and wrestling, five to seven for most of the rest. But each Ivy League college fields something like thirty-five men's and women's teams per year (Harvard leads the league with forty-one). Taking seven as the average number of athletic hooks per team and adding thirty-five for football, the average number of athletic recruits in an Ivy League college's freshman class would be 280. In the case of Columbia, the Ivy League college with the smallest freshman class, athletic recruits could exceed one quarter of the class.

With these figures as a background, let's take it a step further and suggest that for every ethnic, geographic, economic, athletic, or alumni hook, the slice of the admissions pie left over for hookless kids gets smaller. With fewer spaces available for the majority of the applicant pool, a college becomes several notches more selective, and, as we saw earlier, increased selectivity is the juice that powers a college's image—its desirability for subsequent generations of applicants, its power to bestow retroactive glamour and brainpower on its former graduates, and, therefore, its fund-raising success with alumni. Even its success in selling sweatshirts in the distant markets of Istanbul and Bombay can be enhanced by notable selectivity. (When it comes to peddling athletic paraphernalia, being hard to get into is almost as important as winning at football or basketball.) These factors help explain why hooks play such an important role in college admissions, and why they are likely to do so for many years to come.

But for you right now, the question is, with this hook situation muddying the picture of who gains admission, how can you reckon a specific candidate's chances of getting in? Especially if that candidate is you. I believe your best resource is your school's college counseling office. Counselors know how students with similar profiles have fared at the specific colleges you are interested in. Furthermore, they know the context in which students perform, understand what the tough courses at school are, and have a sense of where each student stands. (In this regard, you may be pleasantly surprised with the expertise your school's counselor brings to knowing just how kids stack up in the wider marketplace of admissions as athletes, artists, dramatists, and even piccolo players.) But most crucial, if the college counseling office is doing its job, it is responsible for seeing that each applicant has good college options. We counselors can't guarantee admission to individual schools, of course, but we can shoot for a slate that makes good tactical sense. In this way, our offices are where the buck stops. Accordingly, if applicants (and their parents) find themselves awake in the deep of a winter's night wondering how it will all work out, be assured they are not alone. Their local college counselor is doing quite a bit of wondering, too, and hopefully has helped them get it right.

Another college office resource that can help you discover who gets in is the School Profile prepared by high schools each year to accompany the transcript and letter of recommendation. The School Profile includes such information as the range of SATs and SAT IIs earned by each class, grade point averages broken down by quintiles (fifths) or deciles (tenths), the range of courses offered by the high school with particular attention directed to AP courses and AP test results in each subject, and a list of colleges to which previous classes have matriculated. These numbers paint a useful statistical picture of a specific school. If you go over this information carefully and then ask the college office to give you a list of colleges to which students with roughly the same statistical profile as your own gained admission in recent years, you will know quite a lot about the relative quality (and potency) of that high school in the admissions marketplace.

Also, with profile information in hand, families can usefully consult one of the many college guides that present the statistics for each college's freshman class. College guides range from statistically objective tomes like the College Board's encyclopedic *College Handbook*, to James Cass and Max Birnbaum's eminently useful *Comparative Guide to American Colleges*, to more subjective books like *The Fiske Guide to Colleges*, which awards academic, social, and quality-of-life "stars" to colleges, just like stars awarded to restaurants. Although there is always some room for creative interpretation when you look at the numbers, try not to be dazzled by the rose-colored hue through which even the sharpest and most cynical business executives (who get big bucks at the office for analyzing data) often view the chances of their own children. Beware of the wishful thinking that might lead you to believe that lettering on the high school basketball team automatically makes a child a bona fide college recruit, or that a college admissions officer at a tough place would never be so petty as to notice a couple of C−'s on the transcript. But by the same token, this audit needn't be a reign of terror. If you shoot for an honest and clear-thinking assessment of strengths and weaknesses embedded in the data, the reward is great. It puts a solid foundation under the necessary strategizing of building a college list, which is covered in the next chapter.

I have found that in many instances, once this analysis and audit is accomplished, families can actually relax. Perhaps this happens because, by pulling their doubts and fears into the light of day, they often find that many of their deepest subterranean dreads are unfounded: things really aren't so bad after all, and when the admissions audit is on the table, there are many more strengths than weaknesses.

16

BUILDING AN EFFECTIVE COLLEGE LIST

A key to maintaining your mental health is to put together the right list of colleges. If you shoot too high by applying only to "maybes" and "long shots," senior year becomes a jumble of sleepless nights, a minefield of explosive pressure that sends kids close to the edge every time a graded assignment is handed back in school. For parents, even relationships with old friends can become testy and furtive, because we fear one of them might ask us point-blank: "Don't you think Kenyon College will be quite a stretch for Matthew?" A list too close to the razor's edge can lead to creeping paranoia, intensified by the sense that no one—not the guidance counselor or the physics teacher who doesn't seem to grasp that a B− can change everything, not even your minister, rabbi, or priest—really understands the deadly awfulness of it all. But if you shoot too low, you can find yourself enduring long winter months filled with a murky sense of unfulfilled promise—like living night after night on cornflakes for dinner because no one can manage to put together a real meal.

Luckily, there is a way to avoid both of these extremes. The first step is to research the available college options carefully and come up with a reasonably long list of schools that fulfills as many intellectual and personal needs as possible. The next step is to use college guides and the advice of your college counselor to arrange this list in order of selectivity. As you list the colleges, jot down the test score average, grade point average, and/or class rank in quintiles next to each name (e.g., Barnard College: 670V-620M, 3.7 GPA, 94% in top quintile).

The third step is to figure your own academic-extracurricular profile. First of all, establish your grade point average. If your high school does not rank (and many, especially private schools, do not), try to determine which quintile you fall into by using your school's profile or by asking your school counselor. Then write down your SAT scores. If you have taken the test more than once, choose your highest verbal score and your highest math score. (If instead of the SAT you have taken the ACT several times, choose your best sub-scores). The reason it's okay for you to choose your best scores is that these are the ones colleges will use, not simply because they are lovely people, but because they want the best scores for the data *they* will send to various rating guides in the future.

Although we have all heard talk about the diminishing impact of SAT scores in the admissions process (see chapter 13) and some two hundred colleges have even made score submission optional (or have made it possible to substitute a slate of SAT II scores instead of SATs), the fact is that SATs still count. That is because, as I have already mentioned, a selectivity hierarchy based almost exclusively on grades and test scores still drives the admissions market.

This hierarchy has to be based on something, and whether or not scores are truly useful predictors of college success is beside the point when scores are so convenient and memorable for fixing colleges in a pecking order. In fact, score-based rankings are so ingrained that even families who hate SAT scores when applied to their own kids turn around and quote them as gospel when choosing colleges. Accordingly, I have seen dozens of families in my office every year who in one sentence bemoan the role that test scores play in admissions and then in the next refuse even to consider colleges that don't show high enough test score averages to suit them.

But college admissions officers are not just fools for high scores. Through the bitter experience of quickie flunk-outs, they know the best predictor for future failure in college is the combination of high test scores and low grades—the portrait of the classic underachiever.

When you have put scores and grades together (e.g., 540V-550M, 3.2 GPA, 3rd quintile), you will find it is a combination that you can easily match against a college's profile. What you do next is slide your numbers down the list of colleges you have already assembled until you have located a "comfort zone" in which your combined grades and scores roughly match up with the grades and scores you have compiled for colleges. What we are shooting for is a slightly better than 50% chance of admission for those colleges in the zone. Once you have found this application comfort zone, all you have to do is look a few notches above for the workable long shots and a few notches below for what should be reassuring safeties.

When you have accomplished this piece of figuring, you can relax. You have won the most ticklish part of the admissions game. Now in February when some dog barks in the night or a dream stirs you into wakefulness, you can briefly review the security of the list you have fashioned. It is a list built from colleges that reflect your own inclinations and your own research; you have found its warm and fuzzy center; you have workable options on either side that will buffer you from bad luck, yet at the same time will keep your fondest hopes alive. Instead of walking a skinny tightrope of unrealistic dreams, you've put Broadway under your feet.

To present the idea more graphically, let's try a few cases. Here is a list of medium to large research universities, roughly ordered in terms of selectivity:

Yale University
Brown University
Cornell University
University of Pennsylvania
_____

The Johns Hopkins University
University of Chicago   *Comfort Zone*
University of Michigan
Washington University
_____

University of Wisconsin
University of Rochester
Tulane University

Boston University
George Washington University
University of Pittsburgh

Now let's say our theoretical applicant, we'll call him Tim, has a grade point average of 3.7, which puts him in the middle of the first quintile of a medium-sized suburban high school. His transcript is solid and includes a couple of AP courses (one of which is calculus), four years of French, and two years of laboratory science. His SATs are 670V/680M and he has three SAT IIs in the low 600s. Tim is active in a number of extracurricular activities and lettered on the varsity baseball team as a junior, but he probably won't be recruited by college coaches. He will need a modest amount of financial aid.

With these components in mind, Tim's comfort zone falls between Johns Hopkins University and Washington University. Because he has a statistically better than 50% shot at each of these schools, if he selects three to apply to, he should be assured admission.

Now all we have to do is choose a couple of longer shots from the Yale, Brown, Cornell, Penn list and a couple of safeties from the Wisconsin, Rochester, Tulane, Boston, George Washington, and Pittsburgh group. Because the comfort zone has been achieved, presumably to everyone's satisfaction, Tim should be more relaxed about following his heart's desire in selecting long shots and safeties. In other words, if Yale really is the top choice, he should go for it even though it might be incrementally more difficult to get into than Brown. If Wisconsin and Rochester seem like schools where winter might rule too much of the academic year, why not choose Tulane and George Washington as backups.

If, on the other hand, this same Tim is looking toward a group of small liberal arts colleges, his preliminary list might look like this:

Amherst College
Swarthmore College
Haverford College
Carleton College

Bates College
Oberlin College   *Comfort Zone*
Colorado College
Hamilton College

Kenyon College
Franklin and Marshall College
College of Wooster

With this list, Tim's comfort zone runs between Bates and Hamilton. This leaves him to choose among Amherst, Swarthmore, Haverford, and Carleton for long shots and Kenyon, Franklin and Marshall, and Wooster for safeties. Once again, it becomes clear how finding the comfort zone serves to take the pressure off an anxious family.

THE TYRANNY OF LISTS

The problem with the list approach is that it slavishly surrenders to a hierarchical view of colleges resting on the assumption that every student will be best served by the college that is one notch more selective than the college just below it. I would argue that this fine-tuning rarely reflects the realities of actual colleges and their programs, and that a family, when choosing among colleges to apply to, will be better served by looking at the schools on their own merits, not solely at their place on some market-driven pecking order. Furthermore, if you honestly and fairly take this approach, you will be amazed at how close together in real quality colleges on a list like the one above actually will be. A list by its very nature divides things into graphic intervals, but that doesn't mean these intervals are as widely and evenly spaced as they appear.

To illustrate what I'm talking about, let's look down at the bottom of our hypothetical list at the College of Wooster—a thoughtfully administered, well-endowed, beautifully situated piece of campus architecture located in the rolling hills of central Ohio near other fine schools like Oberlin and Kenyon and Denison. About ten years ago, the several thousand college counselors gathered at the National Association of College Admissions Counselors annual meeting were asked to name the college that had recently surprised them with its high quality. The College of Wooster was the hands-down winner. This should have come as no surprise at all, because, as anyone who knows this college will surely tell you, Wooster has long been a school that provides a remarkable combination of academic rigor and personal support to its students. Yet on our hypothetical list, it's in the basement. But that is how lists function, and what embodies their tyranny.

By this point, you are probably sick of reading a chapter that starts by telling you how to create lists and then ends up by lecturing you about how lists can mislead. I didn't do this to confuse you. It's a little like what Charlie Parker once said, "Learn your scales backwards and forwards and inside out. Then throw all that away and just wail." So learn to use lists as tools in the application game and forget all about them when its comes to final judgments. Then make the most of the college you attend.

WHY SO MANY APPLICATIONS?

A lot of parents are shocked by the steady upward creep in application numbers. In my day, they are fond of pointing out, a couple of applications were the norm. Anything beyond that they see as superfluous, a waste of money and time. Although I am sympathetic to this point of view, I can't look back fondly at the good old days, and it's all on account of Mrs. Batcheldor. She was the secretary in the college counseling office at Hackley School when I ostensibly took over its operation in 1968. I say "ostensibly," because as long as Mrs. Batcheldor was on the premises, this fearsomely correct and powerfully intelligent graduate of Radcliffe College in the 1920s would be running the show. Back then the photocopy machine was in its infancy—expensive, bulky, balky, and not yet a staple piece of machinery in school offices. The way we got letters of recommendation out to colleges was that I would peck out a rough draft on my ancient Underwood, clean it up as best I could, and then pass it on to Mrs. Batcheldor so she could type an original for each college. With this system, I didn't limit application numbers out of a sense of either puritan restraint or environmental consciousness; I did it out of the sheer terror of having to ask Mrs. Batcheldor to type another one. By the late '60s, Mrs. Batcheldor had pretty much had it with the youth of the day and their lack of standards—me included. When I entered her inner sanctum to plead for an extra letter, I knew if I didn't prepare my case clearly it could be dismissed out of hand with a frosty look and a single word. A word like "piffle."

Today, no such limiting factors exist. The photocopy machines have come and the Mrs. Batcheldors have gone—and with her passing so, by and large, has the word piffle. But the advent of photocopy machines is not the only reason students apply to six or eight schools. They do it because it makes sense as a strategy. By applying to more schools, kids increase their chances at "near-reach" colleges and in April have more to choose from. Most important, if they are candidates for financial aid, they have a greater chance of getting a better award. In other words, preparing six or eight or even ten applications is expensive; it is time consuming; it is a waste of paper and sanity—but it works.

PART 5

TAKING CONTROL
OF THE APPLICATION CYCLE

17

APPLYING WELL

THE USES OF GOOD PROCESS

I t's been a long time coming, but by putting together a list of colleges to shoot for, kids have learned a good deal. Hopefully, they have worked hard researching various college options, have talked through their feelings and inclinations with others, and are sharpening their own sense of who they are and what roads they would like to travel down. Finally, by doing the hard work of creating an effective college list, kids should have put together a set of insights (tools, really) that will make them more powerful applicants. In specific terms, this good process means that:

1. They will know the strengths of the colleges they have chosen and be able to discuss the opportunities each affords them.
2. The snug statistical matchup that exists between themselves and their colleges will turn them into comfortable, nonfrazzled applicants.
3. This comfort level will in turn enable them to write essays from the heart. Rather than serving up warmed-over renditions of what they think colleges want to hear, their words will be filled with an original spark.
4. Unencumbered by the sense of inadequacy that haunts so many kids throughout the application process, they will be at their best when they talk with college or alumni interviewers.
5. Because of their thoughtful approach, their relationship with the school's college counselor will be based on collaboration and trust.
6. They will earn the respect of their teachers and peers as well-informed copers, not magical dreamers in search of a statistical miracle.
7. If they are knowledgeable about what each college on their list has to offer in the way of intellectual enrichment and social growth, when it comes to final choice, they will feel less overwhelmed by prestige factors, which often seem like the only compass points guiding many of their friends.
8. They will discover that the very process of analysis they have used is a step toward the ultimate by-product of the college admissions process: taking charge of their lives.

9. Parents, seeing all this positive activity, will ease up and begin giving their child the respect and autonomy that he or she has earned.

10. For everyone concerned, the winter ahead will still have its chills, but it need not have so many thrills.

18

JUMP-STARTING THE APPLICATION

Talk to almost any applicant or parent when their admissions saga has finally drawn to a close and they will tell you the real nightmare was meeting deadlines. Even kids who are regularly good about handing in schoolwork on time have been known to fail utterly when it comes to getting a grip on college applications. In extreme cases the difficulties go far beyond simple procrastination. It's almost as if some twisted scientist from a grade-B, black-and-white sci-fi thriller had snuck into their room at night and with a giant syringe withdrawn every vital and useful fluid from their bodies, turning them into catatonic slugs with bad attitudes.

Of course, there are good reasons to delay admissions paperwork. No one likes to be audited and nobody likes to lose, especially as publicly as seems to be the fashion with college admissions these days. But rather than dwelling on these generalized and well-understood dreads, let's look at a couple of different techniques.

One is simple nagging. For a lot of parents, it's the main strategy, so much so that their kids actually rely on it to light a fire under them. But before you adopt this as a technique, let's consider what is known as the Effective Parental Nagging Quotient. The EPNQ is based on the scientific fact that nagging, if not used as directed, can result in the buildup of resistances and immunities, rendering the nagger impotent in effecting any activity at all and the naggee more dug in than ever. In the specific case of college application preparation, independent research further reveals that total *effective* nag time over the length of the application season may not exceed ninety-three minutes. Because this quotient can be used up in as few as two sessions, parents should be wary of squandering nagging early and then being left with no other recourse but to wander off twitching and muttering to themselves while, as the deadlines march ever closer, nature takes its perilous course somewhere else in the house.

When evaluating the power of parental nagging, another factor to consider is the Bussey Hypothesis. This breakthrough concept is based on the work of my friend and colleague Bill Bussey, a pioneer in asking parents to put themselves in their children's position. As an exercise, Bussey suggests parents try seeing it this way:

Pretend for a moment you are in real estate sales. The market is down and properties just aren't moving. How would you like it if when you came down to breakfast, your kids started bugging you all the time about how *your* work is going. "Hey Dad," they might say, "didn't I notice the Jones place down the street with the Acme Realty sign on it just sold? How come you didn't make the sale? Shouldn't you be hustling a little harder? Making a few more calls? Do you think mowing the lawn on Sunday afternoon right in the middle of the prime selling season is the best use of your time?" Of course, Bussey's point is that if parents thought about how they would react, they might come up with a different strategy for dealing with their kids. So let's try that ourselves.

Okay kids, now that we've got the nagging problem taken care of, this is what *you* have to do. Begin by breaking the task into bite-sized chunks. Starting small and at the periphery of the job warms you up and provides a sense of motion and early accomplishment.

Step One: Instead of pulling out the essays and inducing a bout of depression, work on that mountain of college brochures and applications that has been building up in your room since last spring. By now it's probably terrifying. Why not do an hour or so of basic sorting and discarding? It's physical, no-brainer work, and it will probably eliminate a fire hazard. So even if it takes renting a Dumpster outside the bedroom window, go for it. I bet that before suppertime you can work it down to a manageable quantity. With the old momentum going, you'll feel a lot better, and so will your parents.

Step Two: Now that you know which envelopes you have decided to keep, why not slit them open to see what they actually contain? Then you can go about putting things away in one of those plastic file crates. You will be amazed at how good you will feel when you have each college's information packet scanned and each application in its own folder. It might even be a good time to send out for pizza.

Step Three: On another day you can proceed to the inventory. Do you have the right materials for each of your colleges? This is a good time to find out.

Step Four: Construct a deadline spreadsheet with due dates and check boxes so you can log in completed tasks. (For example, secondary school report to guidance office, recommendation form to Mr. Jones, etc.)

Step Five: Begin filling out applications. But before you start entering information on the lines and boxes provided, organize the information you will need for every application in one place: your Social Security Number, your High School Code Number (the one you used when registering for the SAT or the ACT), your school activities, outside interests, jobs, and so on. You will consult this list a lot, so make it clear and accurate. This might be a good point at which to ask for some parental help to make sure the dates are correct and to keep you from leaving something out. If you apply on disk or over the Internet, the task of entering your data will be greatly simplified. Nevertheless, organizing your vital statistics in one place before you begin is still an important way to keep the details straight and give you a sense of the overall picture you will paint of yourself in your application.

19

SOME THOUGHTS
ON WRITING COLLEGE ESSAYS

Application essays are the thing you're really worried about, right? The nightmare within the nightmare. This is the moment when you're asked to fill a blank piece of paper with something deep and scintillating, yet every time you pick up a pencil or turn on your computer to start the job, your brain turns to cottage cheese. Cottage cheese that has expired. The free-floating angst around school doesn't help either, especially since you're worried that the sentences you are about to compose will alter the course of your life forever. But mostly you worry about having nothing interesting to say. Other kids seem to have lives in which everything ends up sounding like subject matter—such as the girl who visited the Virgin Islands on vacation for a week and made it sound like she was in the

Peace Corps. As if that wasn't bad enough, there are the kids with their own after-school essay trainers who can help them rewrite dumb ideas into Pulitzer-quality stuff. With so much plotting and scheming going on when it comes to essays, it often seems as if they are manufactured rather than written.

The truth is that things have been out of hand on the essay front for several years now, so much so that I was moved to give the following talk to the Middle States regional meeting of the College:

Every year the process of getting into the nation's most selective colleges grows more complex and intense. Back in the fairly recent good old days, students took College Board exams, submitted a high school transcript, wrote a few essays, and maybe had an interview. Now the campaign often begins with a costly program of test preparation, the high school record is often self-conciously larded with Advanced Placement courses, and the lives of high-achieving adolescents seem dominated by the alpha and omega of college admissions.

Recently the college essay has come into the spotlight. Bestselling books showcase "essays that worked," guidance counselors attend workshops on the care and feeding of young writers faced with deep questions, and kids begin contorting their young lives in the hope that clever ideas will flow. As a close observer of the field, I'm worried by the increased attention the essay is getting from the applying public.

Call me naïve, but I've always regarded the college essay as a private space, the place where a student can take charge, be free to speak honestly and directly and perhaps eloquently on his or her own behalf. Until recently the essay seemed like the last sanctuary in which kids could work independently. Interviews are required less frequently, and test scores are tainted by the specter of cram schools. Now it seems the essay, too, has lost its innocence.

The assault on the essay started benignly enough. A college counselor or two suggested that students might do something interesting over the summer before their senior year in high school. It might give them a perspective they hadn't gained in school or by working some "Macjob." And that perspective, these counselors suggested, just might come in handy when it came time to write the college essay.

A new industry in summer programs quickly sprang up to add demonstrable sparkle to the otherwise cookie-cutter lives of our soccer-besotted youth. Colleges opened their campuses to high school kids eager to study all manner of adventuresome-sounding courses in film, journalism, and the arts. And kids started traveling under the banner of their essays, so much so that soon no mountain trail from the Appalachians to the Himalayas was spared the tramping feet of the incipient essayist. This "pre-essay" summer became such a big deal that I thought that in a year or two I would be getting a letter from one of my students that would go like this:

Dear Mr. Mayher,

I want to thank you for recommending Camp Ralph Waldo Emerson. Essay-writing camp is great. When I got up here three weeks ago I was just an ordinary kid. Sure I like school and was doing well in those AP courses. I had a lot of friends and loved my teammates on the varsity soccer and basketball teams and my work on the school paper. But I realized, after people told me how important my college essay was going to be next year, that I would have to do something significant so I could write about it in my application.

Here at camp they make that really easy. And the best part is that you don't have to do anything. They have this machine you sit in which gives you a whole summer's worth of experience. It works like those flight simulators the astronauts use to show them what piloting a spacecraft is like, except these simulate activities that admissions directors think are worthwhile. They call it "The Summulator." So far I've chosen scuba diving in the strait of Magellan, replacing the heart valves in my golden retriever (using materials available at my local drug store), living among the homeless of Rangoon, and accompanying Oliver North on a secret mission. (The Summulator had a bike trip to France that looked swell, but my counselor at Camp Emerson said kids had worn it out so they don't use it anymore.)

Another thing I like here are the Tone Seminars we have every morning. I had a lot of trouble combining humility and assertiveness in the beginning, but they give us a lot of help by showing us how we can combine different personalities to make us sound better on paper. Yesterday we were asked to write about the two people we admire most. I chose Mother Teresa and Donald Trump, and the teacher said I was coming along just fine.

I used to make fun of my parents for taking self-improvement courses and consulting guidebooks before picking up bagels on Columbus Avenue, but now I see they were right. A thing like essay camp can make my life sound just like it's supposed to.

It saves a lot of time, too. When I'm finished here, I'll be able to take a full course from the Princeton Review, and there's an Interview Techniques Workshop where

Ross Perot shows us how to use pie graphs to highlight our accomplishments.

Well, I've got to run. I'm already late for the Conciseness Drills they have us do to aerobic music.

Thanks again for making my summer,

Jeremy

Luckily, things haven't gotten to this point. Even luckier is the fact that, for all its challenges and frustrations, essay writing actually helps kids grow. Accordingly, it is a task that shouldn't be skipped or hired out.

Take the initial problem of finding the writer's voice. It's a killer in the beginning, and in the first drafts kids show me they are almost always contorting themselves into someone else—anyone, it seems, but themselves. Here are a few typical examples. There's the "tiny person" with handwriting so small and clenched that the essay looks like a note smuggled out of a chipmunk penitentiary. Then there is the "humble soul" who introduces every essay with a torrent of hand-wringing disclaimers: "I don't know why you're even going to read this, because I've never been much for writing and besides . . ." Just as bad is the kid who turns himself into a pompous "junior senator" type, thesaurusizing his way through half-baked grandiosities that would make political candidates blush. But probably the worst is the "master of metaphor," who spins out convoluted figures of speech so complex that soon the reader feels painted into a briar patch without a canoe paddle.

One reason kids have a hard time finding their voice is that they don't know whom they are writing for. Not unreasonably, they think of their audience as Olympian, omnipotent, and fundamentally hostile. To deal with such a menace it is natural for kids to invent a protective persona.

But the truth is that essay readers are nothing more than bright, curious, conscientious people—frazzled by the pile of folders ahead of them, perhaps, and probably a little sleepy, but basically open to what kids have to write. They don't want to spend a lot of time unmixing metaphors and trying to guess who the writer really is. They want writers who will speak to them directly from personal experience. In other words, the person they want writing to them is you. The real you. That is your voice. With a little practice, you will hear it on the page, and so will they. Once you have found your voice, all you have to give them is some clear thinking supported by convincing details. Essays need not be based on earthshaking events. You don't have to go bungee jumping in the Grand Canyon or discover a cancer cure to have something to say.

A good technique to get the juices flowing is for you to open your applications and copy down the questions you will be asked to write on. Chances are what you will find is an open-ended opportunity to tell the college who you are in questions that usually go like this: "Tell us something about yourself," "Describe an experience," etc. The best approach to such questions is to write about something you care about, not something you *think* a college expects you to care about. If nuclear nonproliferation is your hobby, go for it. But on the chance it isn't, choose something closer to your heart. Then what you have to say will sound like you and have the vividness of personal experience behind it.

After you have copied down the questions, get a couple of index cards and keep them in your back pocket. As you think about the questions, begin jotting down answer fragments as they come to you. Maybe a question asks what you might remember about high school twenty years from now. Initially, lots of things might occur to you: friends, tunes, discovering life under a microscope in biology class. Start filling in specifics. What it felt like to lug that bag of school books through falling leaves. The sudden dark as daylight saving ends. A late-season tournament. Pulling the tape off your ankles, win or lose. The crash of locker doors. Walking away from childhood games, maybe forever. Wet hair. Stars overhead.

Questions, details. Details, questions. Keep those cards handy, and when it comes time to actually craft an essay, you will have material at your fingertips. The cards will guide you toward the question that will be best for you.

When it comes to writing essays, procrastination is epidemic, and you should expect a lot of avoidance maneuvers on your part. Often when I ask kids how they are doing on the applications, they say they have them all done—everything except the essays. That's when we both know they still have a job to do. The kids who most successfully break through this barrier have given themselves extra time; writing, like any mental or physical activity, needs a warm-up period. Even professional writers feel rusty if they let their work go for a couple of days, so why should you expect to sit down and have whole sentences roll forth smoothly? Assume your first efforts will be pretty much of a grope (and they will be), then you won't have to spend a lot of time feeling you have to defend them to yourself (or to someone else who just might happen to want to read them, like your mom or dad). Another reason to get started early is to make it look like you have the situation in hand and so to keep your parents at bay.

This is your piece of work, so make it your own. Get out

from under the covers, review the tips I summarize in the next section, and get going. You will find that for all the pain and frustration the task of essay writing entails, working through it is definitely worth doing. It will help you develop your own authentic voice as a writer and learn to buttress your thinking with specific details. And when you finally have those essays in the mail, it will help you feel like your higher education just got underway, because it did.

TIPS FOR GOOD ESSAYS

1. Copy down the questions you will be asked to write about before you start your essay. This will give you time to walk around with them in your head.
2. Be open to the tiny mental sparks that will provide the specific details you are after, details that will bring your essay to life.
3. Get some index cards for this walk-around phase, and jot down ideas as they come to you.
4. When it comes to choosing which essay to write, the cards will lead you to the ones that evoke the richest material.
5. Write in your own voice.
6. Be careful about openers. Your reader plans to spend three and a half minutes with this essay. Lead into it quickly and cleanly. In this enterprise, less is usually more.
7. Assume your first draft will be a (very) rough draft.
8. Expect to rewrite.
9. Show your draft to a sympathetic (literate) friend, parent, or teacher for feedback. Take their criticism gracefully and get back to work. But be careful about enlisting too many critics (and viewpoints).

10. Get going on the project far enough ahead (do I hear the sound of chuckling?), so you can put it aside for a day or so to gain perspective and have time for more rewriting. Learning how to mess around with a draft is when you will really learn how to write.

11. Be very careful about grammar and spelling. In addition to showing who you are as a person, your essay will show who you are as a writer and thinker.

12. For all the pressure you feel, try to have fun with this. It's your chance to say your piece.

20

THE EARLY DECISION DECISION

As you approach the question of whether to apply Early Decision (the program in which candidates apply to a specific college in the late fall or early winter and then, if admitted, are honor-bound to matriculate), you may quickly find yourself on the horns of a dilemma. On the one hand, Early Decision currently seems to give applicants an edge; on the other, a commitment to enroll made in the late fall of senior year often seems premature—in several senses of that term.

So let's go through a few cases to get a feel for how things can play out. First, there is Melissa. In our talks last spring and in the fall of her senior year she has been all over the place about what sort of school she is interested in. One week it's Penn, then it's the University of Michigan, and the next week it's Wesleyan. Melissa is a bright, imaginative girl, and each time I see her she shows me she is fully capable of making a case for the latest in what is seeming like little more than a disparate group of picks-of-the-week. So when we get together on October 27th to revisit the question (again), I ask if she isn't getting a bit frantic about finding an Early Decision college to love. She blurts out that of course she is, because she *has to* apply early somewhere—and there are only a couple of weeks left for her to know where that will be. When she says this, I pick up on the phrase "has to," and she goes on to tell me about the pressure she feels from her classmates to "go early." She reminds me about last year, when so many kids got into their "reach" colleges early. Later in the spring, classmates with even better records were denied at these same colleges because the slots were already full. She also reminds me (as if I needed reminding) that all over the school there is a gold-rush mentality, with kids saddling up and heading out for the good college diggings before all the nuggets are gone. And it doesn't help when Josh from the student newspaper comes around with a clipboard to find out, for an article he is writing, where his classmates are applying early. For Melissa the rush is on, and she doesn't want to be left behind.

I know a lot of what she says is true. In the past five years the Early Decision market has accelerated alarmingly, because many admissions directors, understandably worried by declining yield percentages as students apply to more and more colleges, have opted to take more students early. To them the arithmetic is simple: supposing a 25% yield, a college can accept one applicant in December and be sure to have that student in next fall's freshman class, or it can take four in the spring and hope to get one of them to enroll. Given these numbers, it is increasingly tempting for colleges to stretch a little when it comes to Early Decision—to go for students who roughly fall into the range of kids they have accepted in the past—even if it means they might have to forego slightly more attractive candidates in the Regular Admissions pool.

In this annual fall scramble that so frequently pits class-mate against classmate and neighbor against neighbor, such tactical considerations weigh heavily indeed. But at the same time it is important to help Melissa (and her parents hovering in the background) understand the implications of rushing into romance with a college just for the sake of beating the admissions odds. She needs to feel that she isn't selling herself short for a better deal—like buying a sweater she doesn't really like because it happens to be on sale. In fact, some of the least happy kids I have known over the years ultimately felt they had pushed themselves (or had been pushed) into a less than ideal long-term situation for the sake of a short-term gain. In April, when their friends are sampling a buffet of acceptance options, it can be agony for them if they feel stuck with something they opted for prematurely. So as I talk to Melissa, I want her to make certain how she feels, deep down, about being locked in early. If she has too many second thoughts about "her col-lege," maybe she should slow down and at least wait for the second round of Early Decision in January (assuming the college has this option) before she plunks down a binding application. After all, college is a pretty expensive sweater to wear for four years if it doesn't fit right.

· · ·

Another Early Decision quester is Jimmy. His record is very good, but not quite the top. To close that gap, he wants to go Early Decision at Dartmouth. Like Melissa, he's heard that colleges make it a lot easier early, and he wants to use that extra bit of leverage to increase his chances. And this logic is fine—except for one thing. The extra leverage, the bump, an applicant gets from committing to Early Decision is inversely proportional to that college's yield percentage: the higher the yield, the smaller the bump. In other words, high-yield colleges like Dartmouth aren't as eager to nail down applicants as colleges with low yields, because they don't have to. They know they will get at least half of the students they accept in the spring, so they aren't likely to think Jimmy is doing them any great favor by applying early, and in return they probably won't do him any great favor by stretching to take him. Therefore, when trying to figure what sort of bump you might or might not get from going Early, look at a college's yield percentage for clues.

When it comes to Early Action (programs that respond early but *don't* demand a commitment to enroll if accepted), yield still plays a role. In fact, Early Action was invented by the highest yielder of them all: Harvard. With over 70% of its admits ultimately enrolling, Harvard hardly needs further guarantees that kids will choose it. And as far as the other colleges that have Early Action programs—narrowed recently by the defection of Princeton and Yale—they do it because deferring a lot of "earlies," as I explained in chapter 5, showcases their "scarcity" in the admissions marketplace right in the middle of the December party season, thus generating a new crop of applicants for the following year.

Getting back to Jimmy's case: it's likely that an Early Decision move to Dartmouth might not be the magic bullet he hoped it would be. If this is the case, the merit of an early application would seem to rest on other factors. For one, is Jimmy, by shooting for Dartmouth, foregoing a magic bullet somewhere else? For another, if he goes ahead and applies to Dartmouth early and, as is likely from his record, gets deferred or even denied, will this knock the stuffing out of his self-esteem, making the long winter ahead even longer? With these considerations in mind as we help Jimmy assess the risks and rewards of Early Decision, both counselor and parents should go easy and be sure to listen carefully to him. On the one hand, thwarting a young person's willingness to take risks can be, in the long run, just as costly as exposing him to the hurt of an Early Decision deferral. Yet on the other hand, we should all remember that a piece of bad news in December really stings, because it isn't buffered, as hopefully it will be in April, by acceptances at other colleges.

Finally, we come to Jody: a textbook case of Early Decision working well. Jody got started with her college investigation in late winter of her junior year. She visited a couple of schools over spring vacation and then did more looking in the summer. By the time she returned to high school in the fall, she had decided the general college flavor she wanted. In her case she wanted a small, residential school that featured a diverse student body and political awareness; she wanted a college with a decidedly "intellectual tone," with opportunities for her to continue playing the violin and with a good premed program. She had traveled widely enough in her search to be comfortable with the idea of being far away from her East Coast home. Given these interests, it was not surprising that she had boiled her list down to Swarthmore, Carleton, Oberlin, Pomona, Wesleyan, and Lawrence.

As she approached the Early Decision decision, she found herself surprisingly relaxed about her options. At first this worried her, because so many of her friends were in such a frenzy that she thought maybe she didn't understand the situation. But when we talked about which colleges interested her, it became clear that her only problem would be how to choose among so many positive alternatives. Instead of being dazzled by college rankings, she could say to me with real sincerity that she would be happy to attend any of them. Jody had achieved "escape velocity." Rocket scientists use this term to describe the speed necessary to break free of the earth's gravity. What Jody had escaped from was the heavy pull of conventional thinking that holds back students from clearly seeing the true merits of colleges.

When I asked her, for example, how she had come across Lawrence University in her college search, she told me it was her uncle's suggestion. As it turned out, he had gone to Harvard in the 1960s when its new president, Nathan Pusey, had just taken over. Her uncle, a reporter for the Harvard *Crimson*, had been assigned to interview the new president, and Pusey had said that he hoped to make teaching at Harvard as good as at the college he had just come from—Lawrence University, a small liberal arts school in Appleton, Wisconsin. Her uncle had never forgotten that remark, and when Jody expressed an interest in Midwestern colleges, he suggested she take a look. Upon visiting Lawrence, she discovered a school that provided not only interesting independent research opportunities to its students but an outstanding music conservatory as well. By discovering a "safety" college that fulfilled her needs and desires so completely, Jody found smooth sailing as she approached the question of whether to go Early Decision—there was no way she could lose. And when she finally selected Carleton, it could almost have been based on a whim.

In case you are interested in her thought process, Jody decided on Carleton because—apart from its superlative academics and fine music opportunities both on campus and at nearby St. Olaf College—its location seemed so unique to her. She had grown up in the northeast and had always assumed she would return there to live. Accordingly, a chance to spend four years on the prairies of Minnesota (while still being able to take advantage of the Twin Cities via the college shuttle bus) and get a first-rate education at the same time seemed irresistible. Not surprisingly, she was accepted Early Decision and went on to play the violin in several ensembles throughout her college career, major in religion, and take enough premed courses to be accepted by several medical schools.

Jody's experience illuminates an important theme: if a family of college-lookers does its job skillfully enough, it will discover that there is rarely just "one" college for most of us; that, in fact, those "perfect" colleges usually come in clusters. If we think about it for a while, this is hardly surprising. But it can be an elusive insight, because we have been targeted so elaborately by colleges telling us, in a hundred different ways, that there is only one one-and-only college out there for each of us (just like there is only one washing machine or minivan). If we take this advertising message at face value, it can make the Early Decision decision an unmanageable situation, in which we try to pit tactical considerations against the necessity of falling in love with a single college, once and forever.

That's why Jody's approach clears the air. Rather than looking for a single college to love, she sought out a group of schools to serve her needs. This put her in a position to reap the benefits of Early Decision: she got a nice bump from the Carleton admissions office because she had committed to them, and this made her admission essentially a sure thing. She also saved the expense and headache of a half-dozen other applications.

Finally, to wrap up our discussion of Early Decisions, I would stress one more time that it is panic that is the principal enemy. With a deadline looming and amid widespread hysteria, it's all too easy to turn the Early Decision decision into a scramble for the lifeboats rather than to keep it in its place as one element in a carefully considered strategy.

PART 6

WAITING FOR NEWS AND THEN MAKING THE MOST OF IT

21

FACING THE CHILLS AND THRILLS
OF SENIORITIS

To a college counselor monitoring the comings and goings of a hundred or so high school seniors and their teachers, January often seems like the cruelest month; the angst of it all flows in such predictable channels that it almost seems scripted. From one year to the next, I know to the week when the chairman of the math department, an experienced and gifted teacher with several AP Calculus sections, will stalk into my office during a free period and be off on a tirade about how the seniors in his classes are once again betraying their commitment to the material and to him. Yes, he knows it has happened in past years, but he refuses to be comforted on these grounds. This year is worse than ever; there will be failures, disappointing examination results. He doesn't know why he ever teaches seniors.

As if by clockwork, my next visitor is a girl in the senior class. She has been a fine student, a community leader, and a real sparkler to talk to; but now she is moving slowly, almost shuffling. Draping herself in a chair, she is silent, all the while staring fixedly at a point just over my left shoulder. As far as I know, there is nothing in particular to look at in that spot.

I have been her teacher and her friend for several years, and now I try to wait her out as gently as I can. After a while, she begins to tell me things. She tries to do her work, she says, but she can't see the words on the page anymore. They just blur. Everything blurs and nothing that used to matter matters anymore. She used to love school and the challenge of doing well, but now she can't get started on even the simplest tasks. She's driving her parents crazy. It began when she was filling out applications. Nothing clicked, nothing went into the boxes right. For the first time in her life she couldn't focus on writing, and we both know writing is her real strength.

I probe a little to see if there are specific troubles at home or with drugs, but these don't seem to be problems. She is bored, she says, bored and fidgety and tired. We talk and, mostly, I listen. She promises to come back and talk some more. On her way out, I suggest that just because she has lost motivation doesn't necessarily mean it is gone forever. She rolls her eyes at this, with just a hint of the old humor, and shuffles on.

Next on the list is a popular and talented history teacher, one of the faculty whom the seniors most regularly ask for recommendations. "Wouldn't you know it," he says, "just when I get Kevin's letters finished, he takes a dive—a D on the Civil War test, and he's late with his paper. I just told his colleges, all eight of them, how responsible he is and how much he loves history. Fleeced again, I guess."

The flow keeps coming, but I am surprised to see Danny, especially when he says he wants to quit the basketball team. Basketball has been the glue that holds his life together. He loves the game and all his best buddies are on the team. "What's changed?" I ask. He has trouble making a case for quitting. He starts by saying he needs more time with his schoolwork, but when I chuckle at this, he concedes that he is not making a late run at valedictorian. Hemming and hawing, he finally comes down to the fact that he feels cooped-up during practices, claustrophobic. He knows he isn't good enough to play in college, so what's the use of sticking it out now? We talk about his friends on the team and his relationship with the coach, and he still looks discouraged. I tell him I'll speak to the coach; maybe we can get him a little breathing room.

As the winter ends and spring begins, I talk to a girl who can no longer get along with her closest friend, a kid she has hung out with since the seventh grade. I talk to a guy who has been late to school twenty-seven times in the last six weeks, even though his mother bought him an industrial-strength alarm clock. I hear the story of a girl who backed out of her garage without remembering to close the car door—the one on the driver's side. In all of these conversations something is clearly out of tune; once again, it appears, a deadly outbreak of senioritis is underway. And not just at my school.

When I talk to colleagues in other high schools, they have similar tales to tell. One year when I worked as a part-time interviewer in the Columbia admissions office and talked to seniors from high schools as diverse as Sunset High School in Oregon and the tiny Maimonides School, a yeshiva in a Boston suburb, their definitions of senioritis were virtually identical, and so were their explanations. These kids said senioritis developed when the last grades that counted for colleges went in and they could finally blow off school without getting punished. What they described was essentially an act of vengeance against adult authorities, who had arbitrarily and capriciously ruled their lives through high school by holding the issue of college admissions over their heads. Now the kids were in the driver's seat and they would do as they liked. Clearly this is a persuasive line of argument, especially when repeated by a national sample of high school kids; but still I think they only see a piece of it. To my way of thinking, more complex dynamics are at work.

For one thing, as I said in chapter 6, there is a good deal of emotional baggage piled up around the issue of leaving home. To compensate for the pain of separation, kids and families naturally make a very big deal out of the college question. Added to this separation anxiety, there is the confusion that late adolescents feel at the threshold of their own adulthood as they finish high school and begin college. No wonder they feel like Grand Central Stations of simultaneous arrival and departure. No wonder—even without the win/lose pressure of college admissions—senior year can be such a mess.

Ten years ago, I received a fellowship from the Joseph Klingenstein Foundation to research the phenomenon of senioritis, or "senior slump," as it is also known. I asked seniors at various schools to describe what they were going through and among the responses I received was this one:

It's difficult to pinpoint, but it's a weird period of ups and downs. One moment it can be diagnosed as spring fever: you feel elated, feel the desire to "get out." The next moment you are down, lethargic, lacking energy. The paper you have to hand in to graduate seems to be an impossibility. Whether up or down you feel an overall inability to concentrate. Your mind wanders; you'll think of the prom, of graduation, of leaving your friends. How can you realistically concentrate on "the core collapse theory" with those ideas racing around in your head?

I think senior slump is just a normal part of adolescence. It's part of the transition period from the teenage years to adulthood, and it's one of the only ways that kids know how to deal with separation. After attending high school for many years, no matter whether you have enjoyed it or not, graduation is painful. You are leaving the familiar to go out into the unknown (corny as that sounds). What I think most people don't realize is that senior slump is a deeper concept. It goes beyond ceasing to care about the grades you get on tests and what you are learning in school. And it's not that you no longer care about these things because you are into college and learning isn't important.

You don't stop learning when you hit senior slump, rather you use the fact that the pressure is off you to learn more about yourself. You feel the need now more than ever to find yourself before you go to college. It's a giant mishmash: you have to untangle yourself from the high school years, find pieces of you that are mixed-up with everyone else, collect yourself, and go to college. At the same time you know that you have left something of yourself in that mishmash because you can't find every piece, but you learn to accept this. That's what senior slump is all about. It's not a disease; it's a healthy, normal reaction to what's happening all around you.

Given this potential for mishmash, the first thing a kid should try to do is understand the crosscurrents of senior year: the pressure of school work, the crush of deadlines, the pain of impending separation. These dynamics make organization and planning ahead difficult but all the more essential.

So first of all, try not to take on too much in the way of obligations at school and in your community—even if those empty spaces on your college applications tempt you into thinking that doing something heroic like opening a homeless shelter might beef up your record.

The second thing to get a grip on is competition. Suddenly you may feel that you are racing against your friends over grades, awards, or especially for scarce places in the same colleges. This can be the worst part of senior year, all the more so because there is a grain of truth in the idea that students in the same school compete against each other. But—and you should really take this to heart—you are battling with your friends and classmates for a place on the college life raft much less than you think. Simply put, colleges are more interested in getting the best kids they can get than they are in maintaining acceptance quotas at particular schools. Why else would Princeton take four students from the same high school one year and none the next? In those hothouses of the second guess that some high schools, and even whole towns, can become in April of every year, it may *seem* that Student A is knocking off Student B, but in reality this is less often the case than is widely supposed. And even in those instances when something like that might seem to have happened, it is best to let it go without comment. The road to mental health is rarely paved with jealousy and paranoia about the good fortune of one's friends and classmates.

A third thing that will make senior year work better for you is to behave well when the college news comes in. While others are talking, just lie low. Appointing yourself the local expert on everyone's acceptance and rejection situation can poison relationships for the long term. At decision time, it's as though everyone you know is walking around with a sunburn, so don't be the one rubbing in sand.

The young people who manage the last half of senior year most successfully are the ones who recognize it as the "rite of passage" it surely is. They enjoy the rituals that come along at the end of high school: the yearbook, senior prank, senior cut day, the prom, graduation. They enjoy the stimulating tension they feel as they move from one world to another. Some kids even make creative use of it. Just as there is an ecological theory that suggests that life is at its richest and most dynamic at environmental edges, anthropologists recognize that human culture is most dynamic and rich at times of transition from one phase of life to another. Kids should revel in the "edges" of their own lives. The process of leaving high school and home, for all it's confusion and jangle, can be a time for tremendous personal growth.

22

WAIT LISTS: HOWS AND WHYS

Wait Lists are big business these days. It's great when kids get put on one (instead of being denied admission outright), and it's really great when they get pulled off a list and accepted by a college they want to attend. But often waiting lists are one endless frustration, especially since no one understands how long these lists actually are. Parents, who have been perfect saints throughout the process, understandably want action when they find a child on a Wait List. With the goal so close, they want all the stops pulled out. They want extra letters from influential alumni, teachers, and school heads. And they especially want phone calls from the high school counselor to the college admissions office in order to really get things moving. Who can blame them? After all, they haven't asked for anything special . . . until now. Things can go so far that in one instance a parent wanted to charter a plane to take his son, personal secretary, and the college counselor straight to the Wait Listing college, march this entourage up the steps of the admissions office, and plead the case directly.

All of this might make sense (well, maybe not an airborne campaign) if waiting lists weren't, as I just said, so long—longer, in fact, than in your wildest imagining. Here are some numbers reported recently by *The Wall Street Journal*: Colgate, with a freshman class of 710, put 1,311 on its Wait List; Franklin and Marshall, seeking a class of 515, had a Wait List of 450; and Vassar, seeking 620 freshman, had 300 on their Wait List.

Several factors explain the length of these lists. The first is that, for all of their sophistication about predicting "yield" numbers (the percentage of candidates who accept offers of admission), admissions directors are so terrified they will not get a full freshman class that they have to buffer their numbers with a nice long Wait List. But even a long list doesn't automatically do the trick. Most colleges lose something like half of those applicants offered Wait List status, because students immediately accept offers from other colleges and disappear as prospects. Understandably, this makes colleges nervous, particularly those whose marketing efforts might have temporarily elevated them into a higher selectivity niche. For example, in the Colgate instance mentioned above, the admissions director said he put 1,311 on his Wait List (up from 500 the year before), because he felt the college had attracted an especially strong pool of applicants and he feared the loss of students who would be accepted by Colgate's "upstream" competitors.

Another reason for longer lists is that a group of colleges used to meet in what was called the Overlap Group to collectively determine financial aid awards to individuals. But in 1989 the Federal Trade Commission ruled that this meeting constituted "price fixing" by colleges, and it was abandoned. Since then, accepted candidates are offered disparate aid packages by colleges making independent assessments of the students' ability to pay. This makes it increasingly difficult for a given college to predict who, among aid seekers, will take its package and enroll.

A final reason for uncertainty over yield is that every year students seem to file more applications, but no one knows exactly how many have been filed until it's too late for the information to be of any use to colleges in their reckoning. Because of all of these question marks, waiting lists—about the only insurance policy a college has against empty beds in a freshman dorm—get longer and longer.

But as the admissions season hurtles toward a close each spring, it gets even crazier than this. To help you glimpse how things work in years with lots of Wait List action, I have put together a scenario involving Middlebury College. In this hypothetical case it is early May, and to the Middlebury staff things seem well in hand as the "yeses" roll in. A couple of weeks later, however—just when it looks like everything is under control—Dartmouth, responding to the incremental Wait List moves by competitors like Harvard, Princeton, and Stanford, which have eroded its class, "goes" for fifty freshman. Because Dartmouth and Middlebury share considerable application "overlap," and Dartmouth is slightly upstream of Middlebury in terms of selectivity, of the fifty taken by Dartmouth, thirty come straight out of Middlebury's class. To aggravate things further, another handful comes out of Williams's—enough so that it decides to go to its Wait List. This Williams move takes a few more from Middlebury, forcing it to go to its Wait List. The Middlebury move, in turn, pulls kids out of Colby and Connecticut College, forcing these colleges to go to their Wait Lists, and thus take kids from Franklin and Marshall and St. Lawrence. This mobilizes activity on the Hartwick and Muhlenberg lists. And so, as the dominoes tumble, the hierarchical differences among these colleges— which are much more imagined than real—are further accentuated.

And as if the dynamics of this game weren't crazy enough, when it comes to Wait Lists there is usually (except in the case of a handful of very wealthy colleges) little or no financial aid left over. With no aid money remaining, colleges are forced either to select those students who don't need money or to accept students whom they know they won't be able to fund on the vague hope that their families can somehow (via friends or relatives) come up with the tuition.

Needless to say, anytime a student's chance of admission is linked to ability to pay, it is an agony for all concerned. Admissions officers feel compromised because they can't choose the best applicants, students don't get the chance they deserve to attend the colleges they are admitted to, and parents feel they have let down their children.

With this discouraging but very possible scenario in mind, it becomes even more incumbent on applicants in need of financial aid to choose their application slate carefully, always keeping in mind the fact that their chances of receiving adequate aid will be enhanced if they are among the first students selected by a college, not the last.

SPECIFIC STEPS AND STRATEGIES IN THE WAIT LIST PROCESS

You find out that you "made" a Wait List if you receive an envelope that feels somewhere in between thick and thin. Enclosed is a postcard that you are asked to return to the college indicating whether or not you wish to remain "active" on its Wait List. If you have already been accepted by a college you would rather attend, send back the card with your "regrets" as soon as possible and help someone else get what they would like. If, on the other hand, you want to stay on the Wait List, in addition to the card it's a good idea to send a letter to the admissions office explaining your interest in the school and updating them on any notable achievements since you filed your application. (These achievements need not be earth-shattering to qualify as notable: surviving the winter of senior year probably qualifies.) At any rate, the idea is to write something along the lines of. "Since I was last in touch, I have continued my interest in such-and-such by doing so-and-so. . . ." That should suffice for openers. *But here is the nub of it:* If in this letter you can also state that you will enroll if admitted off the Wait List, then you might nudge the college toward *you* rather than someone who has *not* made such a statement.

This is the moment when colleges need to fill their classes. They want kids who will show up, and your commitment can do the trick. One final thing you can do to promote your cause is to ask the school counselor to call the admissions office to make sure the college considers you a prime candidate as it decides who to take off its Wait List. Such a phone call need not be made before May 1st, because until the college has reckoned its yield from accepted candidates, its admissions officers will be as much in the dark about their strategy as you are. (In fact, they are so much in the dark that most of them don't even bother to rank students on the Wait List until they decide to use it.)

What I have outlined probably seems confusing enough, but the Wait List game has a few other tricks in store. One of these is that you must choose a college from the ones that have accepted you before May 1st, send in your deposit, and actually intend to matriculate, even though, at the very same moment, you are whispering your true desires to a Wait List school—a little like a bride winking at another man as she walks down the aisle. This is what makes the Wait List game a *very* confusing experience—emotionally and logistically— but that is how it is played. And if you find yourself in a waiting list fix, that's the way you will have to play it. You must choose a college and put down your deposit before May 1st. Then if you happen to get off the Wait List, you forfeit this deposit (and let the college know of your change in plans) and send in another deposit to the second college.

Clearly, given the vicissitudes of the admissions business these days, there is no question that institutions need waiting lists to fill their freshmen classes. Just as clearly, these lists are created with a college's interests in mind—rarely an applicant's. Although Wait Lists can be regarded by wishful thinkers as a consolation prize in the college admissions game (and, in fact, some colleges give out Wait List spots in an attempt to appease applicants with big hooks in their alumni or development offices), the truth is that they are often a painful ordeal for the kids (and families) who are "lucky" enough to be chosen.

23

THIN ENVELOPES: DEALING WITH BAD NEWS

t's true: bad news from colleges really does come in thin envelopes. Thin envelopes filled with thin rhetoric—intense competition this year, limited places, best of luck—numbing phrases that don't quite numb enough. For the first time, perhaps, our kids hit a wall that doesn't move for them. They enter a non-negotiable zone alone. Parents are helpless, too. We can hover—we might even shriek—but largely we feel impotent, and this impotence hurts almost as much as the thinness of the envelopes.

As for the recipient of the bad news, probably all you want to do is lie low for a while, and this is what you should do. Injured animals do this and you can learn from them. It is not a time when the world will necessarily benefit from your opinions. So breathe deeply instead, sit out the gripe sessions, avoid feeding the curiosities of quasi-strangers, let friends hug you, find the right music. In these first couple of days, avoid judging yourself or others (or the colleges that accept or reject you) by the pain you feel. As the mail pours in all around you, it is easy to feel conspicuous, but this feeling will pass. The people who love you will love you still; the people who don't will soon be gone toward fresher sources of rumors. If you give yourself time to find your balance, you surely will.

Within a week or so, perspective will start seeping into your very marrow. Perhaps you will begin to see that being denied admission at one or more colleges was the result of institutional imperatives beyond your control. As we saw in chapter 5, many admissions offices manufacture scarcity to maintain a marketing edge. They do this by rejecting great numbers of students in key market areas in the northeast corridor and other major metropolitan areas. Maybe you are one of these—a casualty in a war for next year's applicant pool. You should also realize that this whole over-blown set of agonies happens smack in the middle of life's biggest transition zone: adolescence. How could the reckonings made at this peculiar time in your life ever be based on who you really are, much less on who you will become? (Looking back from adulthood, who among us would want to be judged solely on what we amounted to in high school?)

Within a couple of weeks you should be getting a grip on whatever mildly masochistic tendencies would have you believe that the college that wouldn't have you is, by that sheer fact alone, better than one that will. (Remember the gist of the old Groucho Marx quip: "I wouldn't belong to a club that would have me as a member.")

Now it's time to get going again. Revisit colleges that

have accepted you and rediscover the wonderful things that await you on their campuses. Consider the fact that research shows some of the least successful college students have been the ones who barely squeaked into the college of their choice and then spent far too much of their academic careers wondering if they had the right stuff to be there. It might be early yet to feel grateful for the rejection, but it may happen over time. We should remember the story that Gary Ripple used to tell when he was dean of admissions at the College of William and Mary. Every once in a while in the late spring he would receive a letter or phone call from a parent whose child Ripple had rejected four years earlier, announcing that the young person had just been elected Phi Beta Kappa at another college. The parent, of course, expected Ripple to feel chagrined at this news, and he would often mumble something about imperfections in the system. But inwardly, knowing a young person had gone on to a great triumph, Ripple would think to himself that maybe the system wasn't working so badly after all.

Research also shows—contrary to conventional wisdom—that where you go to college is nowhere near as important as what you do when you get there, *even in terms of earnings.* A paper by Estelle James, Nabeel Alsalam, Joseph C. Conaty, and Duc-Le To, entitled "College Quality and Future Earnings: Where You Should Send Your Child to College" and published in the *American Economic Review,* arrives at conclusions that may surprise you. After exhaustive statistical analysis of the national longitudinal study of the high school class of 1972, James et al. report that "While sending your child to Harvard appears to be a good investment, sending him to a local state university to major in engineering and take lots of math and preferably attain a high GPA is an even better private investment. Apparently what matters most is not which college you attend, but what you did while you were there. In fact these college experience variables explain more of the variance [in earnings] than measured family backgrounds, ability, and college characteristics combined . . . Regardless of which variables are in the model, measured college effects are small, explaining one to two percent of the variance in earnings."

Another way to deal with your situation is to realize that, although you were not able to control the admissions decision that was passed down to you, you have total control over your response to that decision. With this admissions business in the rearview mirror at last, you can take control of your life. Your future is up to you.

Perhaps you will use the setback as a springboard for greater efforts ahead. Maybe it will allow you to turn your college admissions journey into a story. Your tale might begin with a review of your steps and missteps, or with the agony and hilarity of teaching your parents how to behave on group campus tours. You might remember the Thanksgiving dinner when your family's curiosity about your college plans made you feel more thoroughly carved than the turkey. Drawing toward the story's conclusion, you can tell people what use you plan to make of your education; who you are and what you intend to become. And when it's over, maybe it won't end up being a story about where you didn't get in after all. Finding a way to tell this story can be a powerful process, so powerful, in fact, that the growth and depth I have seen achieved by kids initially disappointed by college news has made me wish that some of those who got only thick envelopes could have received at least one thin one.

PART 7

SOME FINAL THOUGHTS

24

AND NOW, AN ALTERNATIVE

Here is the standard take on college admissions these days: "It's a dog-eat-dog world out there already, and the future looks even worse. There's accelerating technology, depersonalization in the workplace, downsizing, outsizing, and a global economy. So unless kids just happen to want to shovel french fries into little paper bags or do lube jobs every seventeen minutes, they'd better have the right kind of ticket to get them through the big doors to where the real jobs are. And those tickets will be based on educational credentials: college names."

For all the logic embodied in this view, there is a set of intriguing options that might surprise you. It might even put the whole prestige business on its ear. What I'm talking about is a group of evening programs at some of the nation's most august universities: Harvard, Columbia, Penn, and several others. They provide access to institutions on an *open enrollment* basis. To get into Harvard, for example, there are no required SATs, class rankings, or essays. All you have to do is be inventive enough to find out about it, be hungry to get educated, and show up on time for class. And when you do show up, you'll find a faculty that loves to teach the eclectic, highly motivated students who comprise the extension enrollment. This is no second-rate bunch of teachers either. Well over half of them are members of the Harvard faculty and the rest are specialists in their respective fields at other Boston area institutions.

If you wonder whether the classes will be interesting, I can say from personal experience that taking a college course at Harvard Extension with people of all ages and from all walks of life is not just interesting, it is thrilling. One year, for example, I took the History of the War in Vietnam. I was teaching a high school course on that war for the first time, so I had a lot to learn. But more important, I thought it would be interesting and fun to get another teacher's approach and the points of view of adult students. I certainly wasn't disappointed. My fellow students included several Vietnam veterans, a diplomatic correspondent from *The Christian Science Monitor*, an ex-nun who had opposed the war twenty years earlier, several political conservatives who regarded our abandonment of South Vietnam as a shameful sellout, and a handful of early twenty-somethings who had no personal history with the war but were all ears and asked wonderful questions. The lectures were stimulating and the discussions as fascinating as they were unpredictable. I learned a lot and became more open to disparate points of view. This helped immeasurably when I taught the course.

Another testimonial comes from a young woman I know who took premed courses at Harvard Extension immediately after finishing an undergraduate degree at Harvard College. After chemistry class one evening, she fell into a conversation with her teacher about the differences between the College, where he taught during the day, and the Extension. He told her that Harvard College was great, but he often found that as a group its premed students were somewhat predictable and entitled. This made him value the lively scene—the real pageant of differences—at Harvard Extension, especially since he felt his students at night were just as good, or better, at chemistry than his day students. As he was saying this, they both recalled her lab partner from Revere Beach, the one with the nose jewelry and all the great questions. When this kid from Revere got off the subway in Harvard Square with her notebooks stuffed in a gym bag and a wad of gum going like mad in her mouth, they just bet that her fellow riders would be surprised to learn where she was headed and how well she was doing.

In another course I audited on the history of the Middle East, I sat next to a Vietnamese woman. During the fifteen-minute break in the lectures, she would tell me about her experiences in the war that had torn through her country and her life. Just before the fall of Saigon, she had escaped to America with her surviving children, where she had launched a successful produce business and educated her sons. Now she felt it was her turn to live a little, and the way she chose to do this was to take Harvard Extension classes at night, studying anything and everything that interested her.

Although these stories are all very interesting, you might be thinking there is a catch in here someplace, something like tuition. But that's another surprise about Harvard Extension, it's a real bargain. In the 1996–1997 academic year, a four-unit course cost $375. Four courses, the equivalent of fulltime at Harvard College, is only $1,500 per semester, or $3,000 per year, compared to $10,623 per semester, or $21,247 per year, at Harvard College. By going at night, you can save $18,247 per year.

Another objection you might raise is that Harvard Extension is not the "real thing" but a counterfeit experience that could get a person into big trouble down the line with an employer. To check out this line of reasoning we'll try a possible scenario. Let's say in creating your résumé before you got your present job you did not draw a distinction between the Harvards. When it came to listing your college degree you simply wrote Harvard, ALB, which is what it says on your diploma. But now you have just been "caught" and find yourself standing in front of the boss's big desk, being asked to explain where, exactly, you went to college. She thought she'd hired a genuine Harvard person and now she thinks she's got something bogus on her hands. In this tight spot, what have you got to say for yourself?

Your first line of defense is to explain that the Harvard you went to is genuine: same courses, same buildings, same professors, same graduation ceremony, same university name on your diploma, same hard work. What you earned, you earned fair and square.

While this sinks in, you go on to explain the tuition savings involved and what this meant to your family; particularly because it allowed you to work during the day for Peregrine Software in Cambridge to cover tuition and living expenses. Then you remind her that it was precisely this work experience at Peregrine that led her to hire you in the first place. By now she is interested in your line of reasoning and is coming to regard you not as an impostor, but as a person of considerable gumption; just the kind of employee she wants working for her.

Here's another story. It's not a scenario; this really happened. A couple of years ago a recent Noble and Greenough School graduate came back to his alma mater and spoke at an assembly about his experiences working in Japan. In an anecdote about the difficulties of finding a job over there, he told of sitting nervously while a potential Japanese employer scanned his résumé. It was clear to him that the interviewer had never heard of the small New England college—as I remember, it was Amherst—where he had earned his undergraduate degree. But then the businessman noticed an economics course from Harvard he had taken at night. "Ah! Harvard!" he exclaimed, and the young man landed the job. In Tokyo, it seems, employers don't split hairs; to them Harvard is Harvard. Throughout Asia and, one might well assume, for much of the world outside of Route 128 (the Boston equivalent of the Beltway), this will arguably be the case. Harvard will be Harvard (or Columbia, Columbia). Looked at in this way, the only thing that might shock us is that prestige, the thing people say they "need" most from college, might not be as scarce a commodity as we have all been led to believe.

In spite of this logic and the foregoing testimonials, we all know that night school in the midst of a large metropolitan area might not necessarily be the best thing for every recent high school graduate. Regardless of the arguments in favor of such a strategy, many of our kids will need more seasoning in the supportive environments of colleges specifically geared to people in the eighteen-to-twenty-four age range before they set out on their own. They may well need the opportunities for community these colleges afford; they may need the chances for leadership that intercollegiate sports and campus-based clubs and activities provide. Certainly there is nothing wrong with coming to understand this. In fact, understanding the real needs of our kids shows us how complex the process of matching a given student with a given college can be. If we can use Harvard Extension as a metaphor to get us beyond bottom-line notions that can short-circuit real thought, maybe we are getting somewhere.

At the beginning of this chapter, we saw that what most people demand from college is prestige. The Harvard Extension example shows how a family can get prestige at a bargain price. It shows how the appearance of a thing doesn't have to matter more than the thing itself. If parents (or their children) object to the model I have presented, is it possible that prestige is not the only thing they are after? Is it possible that their goals are more complex than they originally stated? Isn't this a good moment to reexamine the priorities in a student's education? Instead of remaining obsessed with a single, overriding factor like prestige, wouldn't we be better off helping our children stay focused on the transformative power of their own educations?

25

EDUCATION BY PATCHWORK

Dick Baker, the head of Noble and Greenough School, used to begin an annual talk to parents of seniors by saying he thought that most, if not all, of their children should take a year off before starting college. His remarks could have been shocking to parents in the last throes of tuition payments to a school whose ostensible mission was college preparation, so Baker was careful to point out that while he felt most of the graduates might be ready for college in purely academic terms, he believed that seasoning in the world beyond school couldn't help but make them better able to take advantage of their college educations. College, he often repeated, is too expensive to waste on someone who isn't ready for it.

His remarks were based on personal experience—he

himself had spent a year in England immediately after high school—and on professional observations made during a thirty-year career in education. A key point for Baker is that people do their best when they believe they have choices. Even the illusion of choice is yeasty stuff. Most of us know that high school can be an assembly line for kids—Spanish III to the Spanish-American War to Spanish rice for lunch, etc., etc. The high school to college to graduate school continuum can seem like that too, if kids don't feel they have any choice in it. A real straitjacket. If we can break this circumscribed pattern and provide kids with some open territory and some "ifs" to chase after, we can't help but empower them.

Baker would go on to say that young people are naturally ambivalent about their futures, especially about whether they will measure up or not. Doing something out of the ordinary—something that doesn't necessarily "count" on the school-to-career conveyor belt—gives them confidence and provides perspective on their own educational process. He doesn't worry so much about the specifics of a year-off program. What matters is the sense of newness and the chance to make choices. If kids can leave home and free themselves from the infantalizing pull of the day-to-day parent-child nexus, that's good. If they can learn concrete skills or participate in the creation of a demonstrable product, even better. Because Baker feels that a high school education, obsessed as it is with the development of testable quantitative and verbal skills, often fails to build other critical intelligences or just plain street smarts. Who knows, the right year-off situation might even help young people crawl out of the youth-culture soup.

One of the puzzling aspects of this century is that with each succeeding generation Americans seem less ready to grow up and become adults. Most current-day parents settled into careers later than their parents did, and they, in turn, went to work later than their parents. In fact, some historians claim that in the eighteenth and nineteenth centuries, a specific in-between stage called adolescence hardly existed. There were children and then there were adults.

In this day and age things have changed. Stages of late, later, and latest adolescence go on forever. We send our kids off to college at eighteen thinking they're grown up and on their own, and they call us from their dorm rooms more in a single week than we called our parents in a whole semester. And when they come back home again at twenty-two—for perilous months or in some cases years—they seem younger and less ready to come to terms with the world than they did when they left in the first place. To hear some parents describe the habits of these oversized, molting creatures—who have re-invaded their former bedrooms and taken permanent possession of the couch and the remote control—about the only thing their kids learned to appreciate in college is a washing machine that doesn't call for coins.

Although I overstate the case here to gain your attention, it seems reasonable to suggest that we look at the ages between eighteen and twenty-six not as a series of discrete, linear stops—college, graduate school, job, marriage, parenthood—but as a single unit of development; a *patchwork* of experiences, which comes into focus as a whole if viewed from the proper distance.

GETTING STARTED

When we look toward the creation of our patchwork, one of the first things we have to do is to give up the idea that it must be dominated by a single institution. It's not the old days anymore. The concept of college as club, for all its charms, is pretty well obsolete. I once had a Boston acquaintance who joked that his grandparents hadn't known people with vowels at the end of their names or anyone who lived as far west as Worcester. When these grandparents went to college, they did so with people decidedly of their own kind. The nation's economy was just maturing and its natural resources and industrial capacities were apparently limitless. In this turn-of-the-century world, college graduates amounted to a tiny percentage of the population, and professions like law and medicine were just becoming formally licensed. Naturally, this minute minority of white males, graduating from colleges established in preceding centuries, tended to work closely together as they went about directing the harvest of the nation's industrial and financial treasure, and, not surprisingly, they did quite well for themselves. Since their era, things have certainly changed, but no matter how obsolete this old-boy network has become—and most of us would admit it's pretty well gone—some people cling wistfully to its simplicity and antiquarian allure. If only they could quietly slip their children through those big iron gates into Olde Ivy's inner sanctum, where they could hook up with J. P. Morgan's great-great-grand-whatevers, they would be assured the best kind of life forever.

Now I am not about to argue that such things no longer happen or, heaven knows, that people don't rely on old ties. What I will argue, however, is that life is more fluid than it was three or four generations ago and that this very fluidity is the mechanism that connects young people with "the best and the brightest" of succeeding generations.

Instead of being limited to the "right" fraternity in the "right" college, if young people look around they will discover contact points and networking grids where they can get to know each other and build friendships and mutual trust. There is, for example, the whole cluster of programs such as the National Outdoor Leadership School, Outward Bound, and the Student Conservation Association. Built around the concept of shared effort in extreme situations, these programs have a unique power to forge enduring relationships. If outdoor adventure is not a bent, kids can look into the community or national service area for urban and rural volunteer programs. Some of these may be private initiatives, some may be part of President Clinton's Corporation for National Service, which pays survival wages and a year-end stipend applicable to further education. In addition to these, there are opportunities for educational internships in fields as varied as archaeology, animal husbandry, the arts, and politics.

Of course, as with any groundbreaker for our kids, there are a few things to keep in mind. We may, for example, have to help them value the relationships they will make along the way, not only with peers but with mentors. Awash in a never-ending tide of their own contemporaries, our children are sometimes careless about friendships that could last a lifetime. We also need to remember that students right out of high school should find adequately structured living and working situations that minimize dangers yet allow them to take responsibility for themselves. This will involve research, and luckily two fine books are available: *Time Out: Taking a Break from School to Travel, Work, and Study in the U.S. and Abroad,* by Robert Gilpin and Caroline Fitzgibbons, published by Simon & Schuster, and *Taking Time Off: Inspiring Stories of Students Who Enjoyed Successful Breaks from College and How You Can Plan Your Own,* by Colin Hall and Ron Lieber, published by Farrar, Straus and Giroux.

For slightly older kids who stay out of college for a year, or recent college graduates with a taste for adventure in considerably less formal settings, there is work to be found on salmon boats in Alaska, or in restaurants or carpentry crews from Missoula to Burlington to Jackson Hole—jobs that will pay survival wages and still allow them to maintain mountain-biking or snow-boarding habits. Of course, there are risks involved, and if mindlessly followed these jobs can become dead-end affairs that erode self-esteem and disconnect kids. Young people and their families should certainly be alert for the danger signs of burnout or the quiet sound of doors closing from behind. But for the most part the rich weave of action, reflection, and learning about a new thing in a new place, combined with the grit and sense of accomplishment captured by tangible achievement, has the power to forge some of the most interesting and farsighted young people one can meet in the nation today. A twenty-three-year-old kid nailing on roofs in Aspen and skiing on the side might not appear to have a lock on some great career, but the biographies of recent entrepreneurs are studded with similar experiences.

Before you panic and dismiss these thoughts as impractical or dangerous, let's not forget the power of higher education to transform and enrich young people's lives. In fact, it's this very faith in the transformative power of education that seeks above all to have kids experience maximum intellectual growth. If young people are dragged through high school and the college admissions process only to be dumped out of the family station wagon in September so they can mindlessly trail other kids through the echoing halls of a college for a couple of semesters before they have a clue about what is going on in terms of their own education, I can't help wondering if they are making the best use of their time and your money.

INSTITUTIONS IN THE PATCHWORK PATTERN

So let's take a look at some of the institutional possibilities. Say your son graduated from high school two years ago. Instead of going straight to college, he joined City Year in Chicago and for a year lived with a group of other corps members in an apartment that is passed from year to year to City Year volunteers. Working with a strikingly diverse group of kids, he helped transform a vacant lot into a vest-pocket neighborhood park, did tutoring in a youth center, and worked in a hospital. By the next fall, the gritty work, the demanding schedule, and lockstep of team activity had him chomping at the bit for college to begin. And it's not just that college looked easier to him than digging broken glass out of urban grime; his curiosity had been piqued by the dose of the world that City Year provided. After that year, it is possible he will never read about the history of the human race or reflect on its present condition without drawing on those experiences.

To continue this scenario, let's say the school he has chosen is a residential liberal arts college. He needs to work on developing his ability to write clear prose and will profit from the small, seminar-style classes and the demand for regular give-and-take. He has second thoughts about the school's isolation (particularly after experiencing a large city like Chicago) and worries that its size might get to him over time. But after talking with you, he has decided that he should take advantage of what this school has to offer initially, then revisit the question of size and location in a year or so. His college features excellent year-abroad programs, and this might be the option he needs. Or he might decide to take advantage of the relatively lower tuition costs and greater depth and diversity of offerings to finish his B.A. at his local state university. There is also, as we saw in chapter 24, the Extension option to consider for both its lower cost and its arguably higher prestige. In a year or so he should have a clearer idea of what course of study he intends to take up. He should also be exploring any number of post-baccalaureate internships and work experiences that have become a regularly required prelude to graduate school admission. If after two years of college he suggests time out to travel or to take a chance at another nonacademic experience, you might not get such a panicky feeling this time because you saw how much he gained from his initial interim year. But then again, it may make sense for him to finish college before taking time off. Either way, if parents and kids can be honest with each other in such discussions, then whenever the tuition dollars are being spent, there will actually be an involved student on the job.

Such a scenario is not a pipe dream. I have worked with countless students who have designed this kind of patchwork. One took some time off both before and during college and is now finishing up as a Rhodes Scholar. Another hitchhiked and walked nearly the length of Africa (this was twenty-five-years ago, and probably a good deal safer than now) before becoming one of the most successful magazine editors and publishers in the nation. My daughter did a service project in the Philippines before college and then worked on a ranch in Wyoming for a year after she graduated. We still talk about how these experiences helped her mature and make the most out of her college education and her career.

FOCUSING

When it comes to the ticklish business of helping early twenty-somethings discover career interests, there are at least two schools of thought. One has it that the way to get young people to settle down and figure out what path to take in their lives is to keep them on the straight and narrow to begin with. This approach probably works well enough, and we certainly see evidence of it all the time. Look at undertakers: it's fascinating to note how many of them are father-son operations. Now it's probable that quite a few little boys don't really want to be undertakers when they grow up, but their fathers take a pretty hard line in the matter and when it's all over, there they are, right up there on the sign: *Charles Smith and Son—Funeral Home.* So we know this way of doing it works.

Another, probably more widely held school of thought rests on the belief that the happiest and most successful adults are the ones who discovered an interest on their own and then pursued it vigorously. They seem like the lucky ones, combining their vocation with their avocation— the people who, as Joseph Campbell puts it, "follow their bliss." If you ask them how they discovered this lifework of theirs, they invariably reply that it came from firsthand experience. This is the reason a rich pattern of travel, work, and apprenticeships in the patchwork makes such long-term sense.

It even happened in my case. Over thirty years ago, during my own year off from college, I visited a basement night-spot in Berlin with some German university students to watch a deranged but charismatic superpatriot perform a dramatic reenactment of the rise of German nationalism. Wearing various historical costumes, he swaggered and shouted about Teutonic destiny and the shattered hopes of the Aryan race, until the crowd slowly came to life around us and began chanting back in an eerie recapitulation of the animal frenzy of the Nuremburg rallies of the Third Reich. It was extremely unnerving for me and my German friends. We had gone on a lark, and almost by accident we had glimpsed the slumbering beast of Nazism awakening again. Afterward we stayed up most of the night talking about how what appeared to be run-of-the-mill beer drinkers could have been so quickly captivated. We talked about German history and especially about whether we thought the fascist impulse was endemic to that particular nation or ran deeper in the human condition. Six months later, I went back to college, majored in history, got the best grades of my life, and became a history teacher with a mission to help young people understand mankind's proclivity both for darkness and for light.

Of course, life is too random to predict such moments of individual revelation. Yet it may be that very randomness that holds the clue. Maybe finding our lifework—and ourselves—is just some giant version of bingo. The more cards you've got down on the table, the greater chance for bingo.

So let's not scrimp when it comes to putting down a full set of life experiences.

Another advantage to the patchwork approach is its forgiving nature. If, for example, one's initial college choice isn't quite right, there are options. If no major seems to compute, a student can take a roll of the internship dice to stimulate interest. And all along the way there will be opportunities to know different kinds of people pursuing different interests in different ways. Who knows which of these might illuminate a new way toward a lifetime of challenges and opportunities?

Which leads us to a final irony: these patchwork designs, for all their apparent variation, might be the ones that bring us into focus quickest. With the patchwork, it is just possible that different college doors might open for a recent high school graduate who, by dint of a year-off experience, makes a new and more compelling case for admission. Graduate school placement may very well be enhanced by the knowledge and perspective gained outside of school. You might get a better job based on some idea or information gained, or because of some connection you made, in the world beyond college. Recently an article in *The New York Times* described executives from major software companies combing the back streets of New York City's Soho and Tribeca districts in search of offbeat cyber talent to hire. Who knows? If you put together your own patchwork, Bill Gates just might give you a call someday.

26

WHAT YOU CAN DO ABOUT YOUR FUTURE

One of the main themes in this book is that a college education should be more than a merit badge. It should be a passport into an interesting, fruitful life, a vessel of developed curiosities and skills capable of moving you buoyantly and safely through the challenges and mysteries that swirl and plunge just out of view at the headwaters of the next century. Relying on ancient formulas based on scarcity and prestige—no matter how tried-and-true they have been in the past—simply may not be good enough.

There is, for example, considerable evidence that "need based" financial aid will soon become an unaffordable luxury to colleges, and that the nation's most prestigious institutions of higher learning may revert to being little more than the playpens for the rich they were before the 1950s.

A recent *New York Times Magazine* article by Andrew Delbanco—entitled "Scholarships for the Rich: Elite colleges are competing so ferociously for desirable students, needy or not, that financial aid for deserving applicants is coming under pressure"—argues that this new era may not be far off.

If that happens, the meritocratic coin of elite colleges is sure to be devalued. If the main criterion of attendance at a place like Dartmouth becomes little more than having a rich old man, it may not have quite the same impact in the status markeplace that it has had for the past forty years. Needless to say, this prospect terrifies college administrators and trustees, and they have raised huge sums to invest in their financial aid budgets to postpone its occurence.

But just to be on the safe side, you'd better begin giving your future the respect it deserves by taking your education seriously. Peter Ustinov once said, "I am convinced that it is of primordial importance to learn more every year than the year before. After all, what is an education but a process by which a person begins to learn how to learn?" With this in mind, maybe the time for you to begin is now.

27

CONCLUSION: FIVE GOALS FOR FAMILIES

1. Try not to sacrifice self-esteem in the college admissions process. If anything, kids (and parents) should feel better about themselves when the task is complete.
2. Learn the value of good process. Applying to college is a complex undertaking. It presents intellectual, emotional, and paperwork challenges and is exacting in terms of deadlines and dollars. Families should view it as an important piece of schooling in and of itself. The outcome in terms of admissions is certainly important, but in the long run perhaps no more important than the way a family arrives at it.

3. Work as a family toward establishing bridges to the adult lives of children. In some measure, when kids leave for college they leave home forever (even if they end up returning for long sojourns). With this in mind, you should work at building ties to their emerging adulthood (no matter how immature they act along the way), because adulthood is the next stage you will share together . . . and it lasts a long time.

4. Help college-bound students learn to give their future the respect it deserves.

5. As much as possible, disenthrall yourselves from the simplistic thinking that so often surrounds the subject of college admissions. Everyone's ultimate mission is to connect a young person to an institution that provides both a scholarly environment and contact with authentic and accessible adults. If this is accomplished, how can a young person fail?

ACKNOWLEDGMENTS

As I consider those people who were indispensable to the creation of this book, I think first of all of my colleagues Joan Danziger at Hackley School and Kate Coon at Noble and Greenough School, whose cheerful and careful listening over the years nourished my ideas on the subject of college admissions as they were being born. Next, there is Dick Baker. Every day he proves that being a head-master is not a lost art; every day he shows that it is the people in schools who are the heart of the enterprise. Not only did he support me with a crucial leave of absence to write the book, but he always believed I could do the job. Throughout the writing of this book, the confidence of my brother, John Mayher, and my friends Joel White and Sam Holdsworth was equally critical. Without the enthusiasm of my early readers Deborah Brewster, Shelley Jackson, and Anne and Maynard Bray, this project might have been shelved before it gained a life of its own. Bunny Melvoin's thoughtful responses to early chapters helped me iron out contradictions and inconsistencies. I am grateful to my teacher Donald Murray, and my student Nina Collins for her providential reappearance. Finally, I am grateful to Elisabeth Kallick Dyssegaard, my editor at Farrar, Straus and Giroux, who seemed to grasp what I meant to say before I had even said it.